The College Girl's
Survival Guide

"I've got two daughters, and I've been blessed that both of them came through college life with a stronger faith than when they started. Hanna Seymour's goal is to make that story the rule rather than the exception for every college girl. Her passion and experience make THE COLLEGE GIRL'S SURVIVAL GUIDE a must-read."   —Dave Ramsey, bestselling author and
nationally syndicated radio host

"THE COLLEGE GIRL'S SURVIVAL GUIDE contains anything and everything a girl needs to know before she starts college. Hanna has the authority to teach this extremely important information to the next generation, and does it in an incredibly relatable way!"   —Rachel Cruze, *New York Times* bestselling author

"If I had had THE COLLEGE GIRL'S SURVIVAL GUIDE while I was in college, it would have had a permanent place on my nightstand. I've been reading Hanna's writing for a while now. Every time I read something she's written, I walk away feeling like I just sat down with a friend who sees me and understands me. This book is no exception. There is a friendliness and a wisdom to Hanna's voice that we all, college student or not, can benefit from."
—Andrea Lucado, author of *English Lessons: The Crooked Path
of Growing Toward Faith*

"This is a book every college-bound girl should have in her backpack!" —Barbara Rainey, creator of Ever Thine Home, author of *Letters to My Daughters* and *The Art of Being a Wife*

"This is the most helpful, applicable, relatable (not to mention warm, funny, and faith-filled) collection of college advice out there...If I'd had this resource back then, it would have been a game-changer for my faith, my education, my social life, my self-confidence, and so much more. I cannot wait to buy THE COLLEGE GIRL'S SURVIVAL GUIDE for every college student I know."

—Stephanie May Wilson, author of *The Lipstick Gospel*

"A must-read for every college-aged woman before her first day on campus and an incredible resource to refer back to."

—Meredith W. Boggs, Nashville-based blogger and writer

The College Girl's Survival Guide

The
College Girl's
Survival Guide

52 Honest, Faith-Filled Answers to Your Biggest Concerns

Hanna Seymour

Faith
Words

New York Nashville

Some of the individuals in the book have asked me to respect their anonymity. Therefore, I have modified their identities and certain details about them.

Copyright © 2018 by Hanna Seymour
Cover design by Whitney Hicks. Cover copyright © 2018 by Hachette Book Group, Inc.

Scripture quotations marked (ESV) are taken from the ESV® Bible (The Holy Bible, English Standard Version®), copyright © 2001 by Crossway, a publishing ministry of Good News Publishers. Used by permission. All rights reserved.

Scripture quotations marked (NASB) are taken from the New American Standard Bible®. Copyright © 1960, 1962, 1963, 1968, 1971, 1972, 1973, 1975, 1977, 1995 by The Lockman Foundation. Used by permission. www.Lockman.org.

Scripture quotations marked (NET) are taken from the NET Bible®. Copyright ©1996–2016 by Biblical Studies Press, LLC. All rights reserved.

Scripture quotations marked (NIV) are taken from the Holy Bible, New International Version®, NIV®. Copyright © 1973, 1978, 1984, 2011 by Biblica, Inc.™ Used by permission of Zondervan. All rights reserved worldwide. www.zondervan.com. The "NIV" and "New International Version" are trademarks registered in the United States Patent and Trademark Office by Biblica, Inc.™

Scripture quotations marked (NKJV) are taken from the New King James Version®. Copyright © 1982 by Thomas Nelson. Used by permission. All rights reserved.

Scripture quotations marked (NLT) are taken from the Holy Bible, New Living Translation, copyright © 1996, 2004, 2007 by Tyndale House Foundation. Used by permission of Tyndale House Publishers, Inc., Carol Stream, Illinois 60188. All rights reserved.

FaithWords
Hachette Book Group
1290 Avenue of the Americas, New York, NY 10104
faithwords.com
twitter.com/faithwords

First Edition: April 2018

FaithWords is a division of Hachette Book Group, Inc. The FaithWords name and logo are trademarks of Hachette Book Group, Inc.

The publisher is not responsible for websites (or their content) that are not owned by the publisher.

The Hachette Speakers Bureau provides a wide range of authors for speaking events. To find out more, go to www.hachettespeakersbureau.com or call (866) 376-6591.

Library of Congress Cataloging-in-Publication Data has been applied for.

ISBNs: 978-1-4789-9357-5 (trade paperback), 978-1-4789-9356-8 (ebook)

Printed in the United States of America

LSC-C

10 9 8 7 6 5 4 3

To my college girls, young and old: Carly,
Sydney, Katie, Maddy, Maggie, Tori, Emilija,
Anna, and Leslie. For allowing me a voice in
your life and enriching mine more than you
will ever know.
And to my catalysts: Abby, Emma, Sarah,
Kay, Taylor, Maddie, and Scarlett. For asking
the first questions and inspiring it all.

Contents

The College Girl's Survival Guide

Start Here

Hello, new friend! We don't know each other yet, but that's what I'm going to call you—my new friend. Because if you read any portion of this book, my hope is that you'll feel like we'd be the best of friends. I've worked with college girls for more than a decade, and one of my absolute favorite things is to settle down with a cup of coffee and talk through the highs and lows of college life—and there are certainly both extremes. While you and I may never meet face-to-face, I hope that you do grab a cup of coffee and that as you flip through this book it feels like we're sitting together having a good heart-to-heart.

Speaking of flipping through, feel free to skip around in this book. Begin by reading the first three chapters. Then the rest is sort of like a Choose Your Own Adventure book, or more like a Flip to Your Actual Problems book. The chapters are laid out by topic, and within each chapter you'll find a handful of the fifty-two most common college girl concerns. You can read what is currently relevant and skip over the rest. Or read the whole thing cover to cover to get familiar with the range of issues that can come up in college. Either way, keep this book handy for the next time you hit a rough patch. Think of it as your trusty pal, always there when you need quick advice from a friend who's been through it all before and who has counseled hundreds of others who've experienced the very same things you are going through!

One of my greatest joys in life is getting to know high school and college girls, and walking alongside them as they investigate and discover who they are, what they believe, and what God's plan is for their lives. I had some incredible older friends and mentors during those years of my life and know what an amazing experience it is to have so many loving, fun, older-and-wiser "big sisters." Ultimately, that joy is what led me to a career working with college students and also volunteering as a high school small-group leader at church. Whether you call it being a big sister, friend, or mentor, my ultimate goal was to help every girl I knew discover who she was, why she believed what she believed, who God is, and who God created her to be.

Now, before you slam this book shut if you're not a Christian—I'm very certain you can still read this book, and we can still be the best of friends. While I've definitely written this from a Christian perspective, I think you'll find the advice on these pages is still applicable and relevant to you. In fact, I hope to show you that when you look at the world through a biblical lens—or the way Jesus would want us to—life actually seems more manageable and makes more sense. So all are welcome here! I'm pretty sure that's the way Jesus would want it.

But back to my girls. As each crop of my girls graduated from high school, I longed to give them something that would truly help prepare them for the next four wonderful and wild years ahead. The more I searched for a great how-to-do-college book, the more I realized how hard it was to find. Many of the books that were written from a Christian perspective seemed a little out of touch or just too old-school. I really wanted to give my girls something personal that digs into the issues I know young women are currently facing while still being written by a believer for believers. But I never found just the right thing.

Still, my girls and I stayed in touch, and I'd often receive emails from them with questions about situations they were facing or things they were worrying about. I knew they would benefit from reading one another's questions, so with their permission, I turned our Q&A into a public blog. Whenever one wrote me an email, I would distill her question into something more widely applicable, then write a blog post that the whole group could read.

Fairly quickly, the girls started sharing my blog with their new college friends, and those girls started sharing my blog with their old high school friends who were at other colleges. Pretty soon, I started getting email questions from girls all over the country (even a few from Europe!) who were all asking very similar things.

The blog was a wonderful device. It united the ladies who read it and normalized the issues they encountered in their college experience. A lot of times we believe the lie that we tell ourselves: *It's just me—I'm the only one who could possibly be feeling this way or struggling with this thing.* But when I posted the girls' questions, almost all of my readers reacted with a "You too?!" They felt encouraged and connected, knowing they weren't alone.

After years of receiving emails and answering questions, I found that all of the college girl issues could be divided into six categories and, even with all their nuances, distilled into fifty-two questions. And that's what you hold in your hand—the book I always wanted to give the college-bound women I knew. More than a decade's worth of college girl experiences, wrapped into one little survival guide.

All that to say, I'm glad you're here, and I hope this helps you transition into and through college. And if you flip through this book and don't see an answer to your burning question, email me. You can always contact me through my website at hannaseymour.com.

PART ONE

The Bigger Picture

CHAPTER ONE

Change Always Brings Challenges

It's one of the most dangerous statements spoken by well-meaning adults, and you've probably heard it a dozen times: **"College is the best four years of your life."**

Well, it's only Chapter One, and we're just getting to know each other, but I'm going to tell you like it is. No sugarcoating. College should not be the best four years of your life. If college is the best four years this life has to offer, that means that by age twenty-two you've already lived the best season you'll ever live. To be frank, that is just plain depressing. You graduate from college and it's all downhill from there? Let's hope for all of our sakes that college isn't the best four years of life!

Even more importantly, the idea that the best four years of your life are in college sets us up with extremely unrealistic expectations. It creates the illusion that college is all good times and great vibes. It sets us up to be shocked when we hit bumpy parts of the road. Instead of anticipating that college will be full of challenges, we are surprised and usually horrified when those challenges come our way. While college is an incredible four-year ride (or maybe five if you enjoy a good victory lap) that grows us in many positive ways—new experiences, relationships, knowledge, and more—a lot of the growth God has in store will come about through really challenging and difficult situations.

There are two elements to understanding and overcoming challenges that I want to make sure you grasp. First, I want to explain the deeper reason why we are so shocked when we experience challenges throughout the college journey. When I came to understand why this is, it changed my perspective and expectations for the rest of my life. Not exaggerating.

I'm sure you've experienced times of transition before. Maybe you and your family moved once or several times while you were growing up. Maybe you've experienced a change in your family situation—a divorce, a grandparent moving in, siblings moving out, or the death of a loved one. All kinds of change happen prior to college that we deal with and grow accustomed to. It's not like you've never experienced change that brings challenges before.

However, the key is that those changes happened to you. You didn't choose those changes. They happened to you, and then you were forced to adapt. Then there's college. Going to college is a choice you make that brings about huge change in your life, and because you make an intentional choice to bring on that change, you have very different expectations of how that change will look. When we choose change, we falsely expect that it will be all puppies, butterflies, and rainbows. Because we feel a false sense of control, we expect the change we've chosen to be glamorous, exciting, wonderful, and lovely. You had the amazing privilege of choosing to go to college. That choice has led you to expect that your life will look a certain way, probably like "the best four years of your life"!

Yet the dirty truth is that new experiences—whether you're thrown into them by choice or not—bring about a number of challenges. This is why, though you've chosen your dream school, you start getting that knot in your stomach as move-in day approaches. You are suddenly anxious, stressed, or even fearful of leaving your high school friends. Maybe you are fighting with your parents so often you forget what it was like to get along. Or you may rush off to college without a worry in the world, but then two weeks into the first semester, you're so homesick that you're already thinking about transferring to the school in your hometown. Or maybe you immediately hate your roommate. Or—worse—you chose to live with your best friend from high school, and now you can't stand the sight of each other. The list of unexpected challenges goes on and on.

Before you start calling me Negative Nancy, hear me out. College is an amazing time! It will most likely be some of the most formative years of your adult life. You will decide who you are, what you believe in, and what you want to do with it all. Yet each semester, from the end of high school to your first year out of college, will be marked with challenges and situations that you'll have to decide how to respond to and transition through.

So don't be surprised by the challenges or the hard seasons of college life. If you don't expect challenges in this life, you will be knocked to the ground over and over—beaten up and bruised by all of life's unexpected hurdles. Instead, if you anticipate challenges, you'll be standing firm, ready to tackle them head-on with good sense, grace, and faith when they come (and they will come).

Think of it this way: You and I are on a beach vacation. We swim out just a little way from the shore, just enough so that we can no longer touch the bottom of the ocean. We are floating along, soaking up the sun without a care in the world, when suddenly a giant wave crashes down on us and we fight for our lives to get back up to the surface to take a breath. But after what seems like much longer than a few seconds, we find ourselves bobbing above the ocean water. We cough, catch our breath, and settle back into our floats. We're relaxing, sunning, laughing—but it happens again! Another wave knocks us down. Over and over, we struggle to survive from wave after wave, never learning to anticipate the next one. That's what life is like when we never expect hardship to come our way.

But maybe it's better if you and I swim out from the shore, relax, and soak up the sun, while still knowing that waves are going to hit us from time to time. We don't fret about the waves. We don't focus on when the next wave is going to come. We float along and enjoy ourselves, but when the wave comes we're not caught off guard. We choose to duck down under the water and wait for the wave to pass, or we gear up for the wave and use it as an adventurous ride back to the shoreline.

Just like we don't need to fret about and focus on the next wave when we're at the beach, we shouldn't spend our lives worried about which hardship might come next. However, as long as we keep in mind that challenges are going to come our way, we won't have to drown in hardship and we will be able to recover much faster!

The second element to understanding and overcoming challenges is this: You must learn to embrace the enhanced personal and spiritual growth you'll gain during seasons of hardship versus seasons of contentment. I believe God uses life's challenges and difficulties to grow us immeasurably more than He uses life's successes and easy times.

When we look in the Bible, over and over again we find stories of men and women whom God uses in extraordinary ways, and all of them go through terribly difficult seasons and challenges in life.

In Genesis, we read an incredibly complex story about a man named Abram, whom God later renames Abraham. God spoke to Abram, telling him to leave his country, his family, and all that he knew, but God also promised to bless Abram, make his name famous, and make a great nation from his line, and ultimately, God promised that every family on the earth (even yours and mine) would be blessed because of Abraham. While that seems like a pretty incredible reward, Abraham had to endure many hardships beyond the first call to leave behind all that he knew. As if leaving home and traveling to a foreign country, without any other details of the plan, besides God's ultimate promise, wasn't difficult enough! Abraham suffered through a famine, having his wife (temporarily) taken by Pharaoh, and decades of infertility (you know he was thinking, *So where is this great nation coming from again?*). And then once God finally blessed him with a child, God told Abraham he had to sacrifice him—literally kill him—which, of course, was a trial of faith. God was never going to have Abraham kill his only son, but can you imagine the agony Abraham faced while he prepared to do what he thought God was asking him to do? Abraham's hardships didn't stop there. Yet God used every single one of those difficult situations—sometimes brought on by God, other times brought on by Abraham's bad decisions—to grow Abraham into a more godly and righteous man. Today, you and I are blessed because of Abraham, because from his son, Isaac, God grew His chosen nation, Israel, which birthed our Savior, Jesus. (See Genesis 12–25.) In the same way, you and I can be assured that God will use all of the hardships in our lives for our good. He uses them to teach us, correct us, shape us, and strengthen us, ultimately molding us into the women He designed us to be.

There's another guy in Genesis, who happens to be Abraham's great-grandson, who also experienced immense hardship over and over and over, even though God promised to use him in a mighty way. Joseph knew from an early age that he would someday be a leader of God's people; in fact, God told him that through two specific dreams. But before Joseph could become that leader, his brothers betrayed him and sold him into slavery. This was after his oldest brother convinced his other brothers not to murder him! Talk about a rough day with the siblings. So instead of dealing with the mess of killing, Joseph's brothers decided they would make some money off of him by selling him into slavery. Over the years as a slave in Egypt, Joseph found favor in the sight of his master and worked his way up to the top of the household hierarchy. But then his master's wife attempted to seduce him, and when Joseph refused out of respect for God and his master, she cried, "Sexual assault!" which had Joseph thrown into prison. Can you imagine? Do you wonder if Joseph doubted the dreams God had given him? Why on earth would God allow his family to betray him, or allow him to be thrown into slavery and then prison, if He was planning on elevating Joseph to a high-level leadership position? And yet God used all of those hardships to grow Joseph's faithfulness to the Lord. He taught Joseph things along the way, through the challenges, so that when he was eventually appointed as the right hand to Pharaoh and given the authority to rule over Egypt, he would be the man God designed him to be—one who would bring salvation to his entire family! (See Genesis 37–47.)

Maybe you already have a sense of God's greater plan for your life. You are passionate about medicine, teaching, or business and have a vision for how God might use you and the talents He's given you. Yet, like our friend Joseph found out, you can be assured that as you travel along the road God has designed for you, there will be major bumps and even detours. However, none of that means God isn't in control or doesn't have a great plan for your life. It means He wants to grow you and give you experiences that will better prepare you for the days ahead.

Let me give you one more example, and this time we'll look at a female friend. In the book of Ruth, the story begins with immense heartbreak and hardship but ends in beautiful redemption. Ruth's family lives in a land where famine strikes, ending in the death of her husband, her brother-in-law, and her father-in-law. The story opens with three grieving women, who are likely starving as well. Ruth chooses to follow her mother-in-law to a country she has never been to before, leaving behind the home and family she's known her whole life. (Sounds a little familiar, doesn't it?) Widowed women were about the lowest you could get on the societal pole. They were poor and starving and had no real way of making money or providing for themselves. I can't imagine the weight, grief, and depression Ruth and her mother-in-law, Naomi, must have felt. And yet God had a plan. Not only did God provide a new husband for Ruth— one who would be able to take care of her and Naomi—but He united Ruth and Boaz so that Ruth would become part of Jesus' lineage. Ruth and Boaz had a baby boy named Obed. (Oh—I forgot to mention that Ruth was infertile for the ten years during her first marriage!) Obed was the grandfather of David, which is the lineage that God promised the Messiah would come from. There were immense hardships and inexplicable challenges, and yet God had a purpose and plan for Ruth's life that took those hardships and turned them into eternal blessings.

And those are just three examples. In fact, you'd be hard-pressed to find a person in the Bible who doesn't experience some kind of challenge or difficulty, but in each of their lives God used seasons of hardship to prepare them for the plan He had in store for them. Why would you and I be any different?

So, when challenges come our way, instead of responding with panic or angst, we can respond with a steady hand, confident that God is going to grow us through the difficult situation. Instead of praying, "Why, God?" or "Please change this circumstance, God!" we can pray, "Please change my heart, God! Grow me and equip me through this challenge. Help me to become the woman you created me to be."

College life (and the rest of your life) will be full of challenges, conflict, hardship, and difficulties. But if you can expect them, instead of being sideswiped by them, and remember that God is using them for your good—to grow you into the woman He designed you to be—you can live a life filled with so much more joy, freedom, and hope than you ever could otherwise.

CHAPTER TWO

Everything Is Normal

I thought it was just me. One of the biggest lies that a college girl believes is that her personal feelings or experiences are rare. You may be tempted to believe this. You may feel alone and isolated. Yet the truth is you are not alone and there is nothing you will experience or feel in college that isn't shared by lots of other college girls.

No matter what you're feeling right now in this very moment, I want you to tell yourself, out loud, "This is normal!" Do it. Say it out loud. I don't care if your roommate is in your room. Say it: "This is normal!"

No matter what you're going through, it's normal. You can't stand your roommate? Normal. You love your roomie and you're attached at the hip? Normal. You just realized you hate your major? Normal. You are desperately homesick? Normal. You never want to go back home, because you love college life so much? Normal.

You get the idea.

C. S. Lewis penned this incredible quote in *The Four Loves*: "Friendship...is born at the moment when one man says to another 'What! You too? I thought that no one but myself...'" Friendship, connection, encouragement, relief—a lot of wonderful things become possible the moment you realize your experience is not isolated. As you flip through the pages of this book, be encouraged. You're going to find dozens of things you've wondered about, and I hope in your mind you hear me saying to you over and over, *You are not alone! Everything you're thinking, feeling, and experiencing is totally normal!*

But even more powerful than finding yourself in this book is sharing your thoughts and experiences with your new college friends. You have the ability to help other girls around you realize they aren't alone. Not everyone will share the same experiences as you, but there is so much power in open and vulnerable dialogue with others. It's amazing the community and camaraderie that grow among women when they dare to be honest about their struggles and hopes.

There isn't a story of anyone going to college in the Bible, but there are several stories of people who found themselves in a foreign land, surrounded by strangers, with only a promise that God was in control. Consider Daniel, one of my favorite biblical characters, who had such a story. I'm sure you know a few stories about Daniel—his most famous one, of course, being when he was thrown into a den of lions and miraculously survived to tell the tale! You may not be as familiar with the beginning of Daniel's life story, but maybe you can relate.

Daniel was a young Jew, probably an aristocrat, possibly even part of the royal family of Judah. During the time he was growing up, an enemy king—King Nebuchadnezzar of Babylon—conquered Jerusalem and took control of the land of Judah, the home of Daniel and his family.

Part of King Nebuchadnezzar's strategy when conquering a new nation was to collect the most talented leaders (intellectual, political, religious, and so on). He'd bring them to Babylon and assimilate them into Babylonian culture—teaching them the language, customs, and history, and even going so far as to give them all new Babylonian names—so that he could utilize those talented folks to further improve his nation (to be the best in the world) while simultaneously leaving the rest of the conquered people behind without any leadership, making them easy to govern and exploit.

Daniel was part of the talented group of leaders King

Nebuchadnezzar snatched up for his own benefit. When he was brought to Babylon, Daniel was placed in an intense three-year program where he was trained in all things Babylonian, including language, culture, and science. He was housed at the king's palace and even had a meal plan! The men in training were all fed the food of the king. Sounds a little bit like college, right?

Here's where things start to really get applicable when discussing the importance of sharing your experience with others in order to find strength and community. When Daniel was carted off to Babylon against his will, he was accompanied by three of his friends, Hananiah, Mishael, and Azariah. The Bible doesn't tell us much about how these boys knew one another, but it's probably a fair assumption that they had known one another their whole lives. It'd be like if you grew up your whole life in the same house, and in your neighborhood were three other girls you spent every day with: You rode the bus to and from school together, after school you did your homework together, and you certainly played when you were finished. You spent every summer day together at the pool, played flashlight tag at night, and had BBQs with your families. Even your parents were friends, because you'd all lived on the same street for years and years. That's probably a reasonable modern-day picture of Daniel, Hananiah, Mishael, and Azariah.

So Dan, Han, Mish, and Az were dragged off together—along with many other young men they had known and grown up with—and when they arrived at the king's palace, they were faced with an unusual predicament. The king's food, their meal plan, as it were, included food and wine that had been sacrificed to idols and hadn't been prepared as sanctioned by Jewish law. At that time, God had very strict laws for His people regarding what they could and could not eat, how it must be prepared, and so on. Daniel 1:8 says, "But Daniel made up his mind that he would not defile himself with the king's choice food or with the wine which he drank; so he sought permission from the commander of the officials that he might not defile himself" (NASB).

It's interesting that the Bible mentions only that Daniel had this conviction. Every Jewish man taken captive with him should have had the same issues—to be a good Jew, to please God, they could not eat the king's food, but only Daniel seemed to be concerned.

Can you imagine the fear, grief, anxiety, and possibly even anger Daniel must have felt being torn away from his home and family and forced to enter the Babylonian training program? Then to add insult to injury, how isolated and alone must he have felt when he realized his fellow Jews didn't share the same convictions he had? Were they not concerned about obeying God? How was Daniel going to survive the next three years if he was already so alone in his obedience to the Lord just upon arrival?

The Bible doesn't say it explicitly, but if we read between the lines, we know with certainty that Daniel didn't keep this concern to himself. He went and talked to his best pals, Hananiah, Mishael, and Azariah. The four of them proverbially linked arms together and asked to be fed a strict vegetarian-and-water diet. I don't know if Han, Mish, and Az were struggling with the same inner turmoil. I don't know what they would have done if Daniel hadn't approached them with his concern, but it seems to me that sharing their convictions with one another created strength and community, which enabled them to come up with a plan and make a bold request.

"Now God granted Daniel favor and compassion in the sight of the commander of the officials…" but the commander said to Daniel, "I am afraid of my lord the king, who has appointed your food and your drink" (Dan. 1:9–10a NASB). The commander was afraid if he gave the boys what they were asking for, they would look weak and scrawny compared to the rest of the group. But Daniel convinced the commander to test the diet on the four of them for ten days and then reevaluate. Of course, God was going to honor His four young men who were risking their lives to obey Him, and at the end of ten days, Daniel and crew looked "better" and "fatter," as the Bible says. Don't you wish "better and fatter" was part of our culture today?

While I'm sure those four young men were great friends growing up, I believe the decision Daniel made to share his concern created a strength and community among them that carried on throughout the next several years as they continued to have challenges with the Babylonian culture violating their own Jewish beliefs. If you've never read the first six chapters of Daniel, I can't encourage you enough. Each chapter presents a new conflict where Daniel and his friends have to rise to the occasion and do the miraculous. Several times, you can imagine it would have been easy for any of them to feel defeated, isolated, and alone, but because they chose to share with one another, their bonds of friendship and loyalty to God delivered them every time.

Thankfully, you and I will likely never be thrown into a lion's den or cast into a fiery furnace, but hardship in college can feel overwhelming and isolating at times. Maybe you, like Daniel, feel the tension of living a life that honors God amid a culture that often lives in defiance toward Him. Or perhaps you have some difficult things going on with your family back at home, and it's impacting your transition into college. Maybe you're struggling with something else—finding friends, getting along with your roommate, choosing your major, feeling confident in your own skin. Whatever it may be, remember that everything you experience is normal. There are dozens of other women on your campus who are struggling with and thinking about the very same things. Find them out. Be the brave one and share what's going on in your head and heart. Remind yourself of Daniel's story—there is power in shared experiences and strength in community. You may even find your best friends through the process!

CHAPTER THREE

Is College a Time to Be Selfish?

"College is my time to be selfish." I distinctly remember uttering those words. As an eighteen-year-old, I left my hometown and headed twelve hours away to a university full of strangers. I wanted it that way. I was excited to distance myself from my high school, community, and family—not because I didn't love them but because I was ready for a season that was all about me. No family obligations, no church obligations, no friends or community expectations that would hold me back. After all, college is a time to be selfish. It's the only four years you get that's all about you. Or so I thought.

A few years ago, I sat through a university baccalaureate service where four graduating seniors shared their stories of life transformation. They were powerful, riveting, and inspiring. Why? Because the heartbeat of their story wasn't about them. It was their story about how God changed and grew them, but they were really just narrators, sharing stories about God and others. While in college, they had been inspired to think outside of themselves and live a life that was outwardly focused.

If we go into college or any season of life with the expectation that it can be all about us, we are making a detrimental mistake. For one, the way you live during your college years isn't isolated from the rest of your life. You are setting up patterns and habits that will carry into your twentysomething years. That means, if you spend your college experience thinking it's all about you, you are highly likely to carry that on into your twenties, thirties, and even further.

Have you ever met a grown adult who still thinks life is all about them? I bet you have, and it's not pretty. Don't fool yourself into thinking that the way you live in college won't have an influence on the rest of your life. Either your college lifestyle will propel you into adulthood or you'll spend the next decade recovering from how you lived. It's your choice. You can choose to be all about you or all about God and others. Choose carefully; the way you choose in college will impact the way you live as an adult.

Secondly, when you make it all about you, you lose the richness of life. When the Pharisees asked Jesus which was the greatest commandment, Jesus responded, "'Love the Lord your God with all your heart and with all your soul and with all your mind.' This is the first and greatest commandment. And the second is like it: 'Love your neighbor as yourself'" (Matt. 22:37–40 NIV). People love to use that verse as an example that we need to love ourselves, but the point of that verse is it assumes that as the selfish human beings we are, we already love ourselves—and to be called to love God and others more than we love ourselves is a high calling. Jesus gives us the recipe to living the very best life we can: Put God first, others second, and in the third and final place, you.

That should be the order of our priorities and heart. And that's not just because it's a great "commandment" and helps us live a good life—it's actually what gives us a rich and abundant life. Life focused on yourself is empty, shallow, and celebrationless. When life is about God's story and community, it is full, messy, and beautiful.

Let me give you a few examples. One of the graduating seniors who spoke at the baccalaureate service I mentioned earlier was a sharp, handsome athlete. He could have easily attended college to play basketball, party hard, and just enjoy life. It would have been natural for college to be a selfish time for him, one aimed at fulfilling his own desires. Yet early into his college experience, a caring professor grabbed hold of him and convinced him to help build an organization that would provide transitional employment for disenfranchised men—those coming out of jail and rehab centers. Instead of taking the easy road, this young man spent countless hours over the next four years launching a nonprofit that spread to include five locations nationwide. While that was certainly a good résumé builder, every audience member who heard his speech knew that wasn't the reason this young guy stuck it out. That professor had seen value in him and, in turn, gave him an opportunity to see value in others. The graduate shared his story from the stage, holding back tears the entire time and often having to stop to gain his composure. His four years of college were revolutionized, he was revolutionized, because someone gave him an opportunity to think beyond himself and serve the community around him.

Another graduating senior who spoke was a nursing major. He went on a university spring break trip to a developing country where he encountered poverty and depression beyond anything he'd imagined. Again, sounds like a great résumé builder. This young man arrived on the scene, horrified and even angry with God because of how bleak and devastated the country seemed to be. He reminisced about a moment at the end of his first day as he was praying, "God, how could you turn your back on these people? How have you forgotten them?" Immediately, he sensed God saying, "I haven't forgotten them. I've sent them help. You." From that moment on, his life was changed. He shifted from a typical selfish college kid to a man on a God-sent mission. His life was now about helping others with the gifts and training God had given him.

*   *   *

My own story had a similar pivot during college. I began as a vocal performance major, something I had spent years of energy and resources preparing for, and by my junior year was burnt-out, exhausted, and empty. I knew I couldn't continue as a music major, but I had spent my entire life preparing for this one thing and I felt completely directionless about where else to turn. While I changed my major to something vague (we'll talk about this more in Chapter Nine), it wasn't until December of my senior year that a lightbulb went on and I realized what I wanted to do with my life. It had taken an older, wiser mentor to shift my focus from myself to how I might use my gifts and experiences to serve others. "Do what I do," she exclaimed. "Work on a college campus and give back to students like yourself. Be a mentor, supervisor, and friend to college students who are looking for guidance!" I had spent the prior three semesters lamenting over what I was going to do with my life when all I needed was a perspective shift. I needed to stop thinking about myself and start thinking about others. My life is so much more rich, full, and meaningful because of the college men and women I have known. While they may point to some things I taught them or moments from our relationship that had an impact on them, I can promise you they have added much more to my life than I have to theirs.

And that is the point. When we turn our focus off ourselves and on to others, we become the person God created us to be—gifts, talents, experiences, and all—and live the abundant life He intended. There is no such thing as a "time to be selfish." That is a lie from our culture that only steals the real joy, depth, growth, and meaning God intends for us to experience. Don't be fooled.

I don't know about you, but I want to live a life that is about God, then others, and then me. I want the messiest, richest, most meaningful life I can have on this earth, and it starts by getting those three things in their proper order.

PART TWO

52 College Girl Concerns

CHAPTER FOUR

First Things First: Precollege + Freshman Year

College Girl Concerns 1–11

> Months are different in college…especially freshman year. Too much happens. Every freshman month equals six regular months— they're like dog months.
>
> —Rainbow Rowell, *Fangirl*

So much happens your first year of college. You will likely have the best and worst days you've ever had in your life this year. If your senior-year self could travel back in time and talk to your freshman-year self, I guarantee your older self would say, "Don't worry so much. It's all going to be okay. Be brave. Make new friends. Trust your gut. Just enjoy where you are."

It's easy to second-guess every decision you've made. *Did I choose the right college, or would I be happier somewhere else? Should I have not pledged this sorority? Maybe I shouldn't have roomed with a high school friend. Did I choose the right major? Maybe taking this on-campus job was a bad idea.*

When these thoughts begin to crop up, I want you to take a deep breath and tell yourself, *I am exactly where God wants me to be.* God knew which college you were going to choose. He knew what you would decide regarding sorority recruitment. He knew who your roommate would be. He knew what major you would de-clare. He knew all of these things before you ever took your first breath on this earth! He knew how your life would unfold up until this point, and even more importantly, He's got you.

God created us with free will, to make decisions, to take risks, and to make mistakes. He allows us to move, make, and mold our lives into the stories we choose, but His specialty is within the realm of His incredible sovereignty, where He uses whatever situation we are in to bring about His will in our lives.

What is God's will for you? It's the same for everyone, and He makes it clear to us in His Word: "'Love the Lord your God with all your heart and with all your soul and with all your strength and with all your mind'; and, 'Love your neighbor as yourself'" (Luke 10:27 NIV). That is His ultimate desire for you and me. He wants us to live life in such a way that we are fully loving Him, with all our might, and loving everyone around us whom we come into contact with.

Are there other nuances and pieces to His will for our lives? Absolutely. But day in and day out, God's desire is to lead you through life where your love for Him grows deeper, and out of the overflow of love He has for you, you also learn to love others well.

So no matter what decisions you make that shape your life and temporary circumstances—like what college you attend, who your friends are, or what your major is—God specializes in using all of those elements to teach you how to better love Him, which includes trusting Him, obeying Him, prioritizing Him, loving those around you, and so much more. Does that make sense? His ultimate will for your life is for you to love Him and love others. He has given you free will to make all kinds of decisions that will impact the road you travel, but the final destination will always be His will for your life.

And we know that in all things God works for the good of those who love him, who have been called according to his purpose. (Romans 8:28 NIV)

That's what "for the good" means. It's not to make you happy or give you what you want in the long run. It's to lead you down a path that helps you learn to love Him more.

Remember, while you may transfer schools, change your major five times, drop the sorority, find a new roommate, and so on, you are exactly where God wants you today. Today, He is using your circumstances for your good. Even if you made a bad decision, He's using that for your good. He's got you right where He wants you.

What about tomorrow? Jesus tells us, "Therefore do not worry about tomorrow, for tomorrow will worry about itself. Each day has enough trouble of its own" (Matt. 6:34 NIV). So stop second-guessing yourself. God has you, and He's got tomorrow covered too.

I'm Super Nervous About Orientation

Concern 1

> "Summer orientation is coming up, and I'm already freaking out. I know I need to register for classes and hopefully make some new friends. But I'm super nervous about staying on campus and trying to find a roommate. Help!"

If you're reading this book before heading off to college, you'll probably soon be attending a one- or two-day summer orientation. I know your stomach is in a knot right now just thinking about it! Let me assure you: It's all going to be okay. Whether you have the best time of your life or you really don't like it at all, I promise it is not an absolute indicator of how your freshman year will go.

Here are four things you DON'T need to stress over (even though everyone else will!):

1. YOUR SUMMER ORIENTATION ROOM ASSIGNMENT.

Most of you will have an overnight stay as part of your orientation experience. Don't stress over this. It's only for a few nights (or maybe even just one). If your orientation roommate is strange, it's okay. If you didn't get assigned a roommate, that's okay too. If you just really don't want to sleep on campus during summer orientation, that's also okay. I promise you, it will not make or break your college experience. If you'd rather stay with Mom and Dad in their hotel room, do that. Seriously. It's not worth stressing over.

2. REGISTERING FOR CLASSES.

Freshmen (and their parents) get crazy when it's time to register. Y'all, I have seen freshmen and their parents in a pool of their own tears. Well, to be honest, the freshmen are the ones standing in a pool of their tears. Their parents are the ones with steam coming out of their ears. But this does not need to be you! ALL that matters is that you register for fifteen to sixteen credits (or twelve if you want to take the lightest, but still full, load). That's it. Your goal is simply to register for enough credits. Don't waste time searching for every professor's ratings online, stubbornly refusing early morning classes, or even freaking out over a general education class that doesn't excite you. You will have time once classes begin to continue changing and tweaking your schedule, if you must. If you are waiting for AP credit to come in, don't register for those classes for the fall semester. Then if you don't get the score you need, you'll just take that class in the spring. It's not a big deal. You are going to have at least eight semesters of college to take the classes that you need, so don't stress over having the perfect schedule your first semester. You will get it all done in due time.

Also, don't panic about evening classes, certain professors, once-a-week classes, Friday classes, etc. I see students bending over backwards trying to make a schedule where they always have noon to 1 p.m. open, or where they have Friday off, or they say, "I can't be in class from five to nine p.m. once a week!" How do you know you can't until you try? Part of the beauty of college is that your schedule is all over the place. Let go of any preconceived notions you have about how your schedule has to be. In other words, don't knock it until you've tried it.

Finally, a word about online professor ratings: Just because Jane Smith hated Professor Apple doesn't mean you won't love Professor Apple. Your peers don't know everything, and you may have a different opinion. Again, don't assume you'll hate something before actually experiencing it yourself!

3. FINDING YOUR ROOMMATE.

Some of you are headed to summer orientation hoping to make a bestie in a two-day period, someone who will make your heart swoon enough to bend your knee and pop that loaded question, "Want to be my roommate?"

Don't do it. Don't put that expectation on yourself. To think you will find a great roommate match in forty-eight hours is crazy. More often than not, I see students do this and then end up loathing their roommate by October. If by some magical circumstance it organically happens and you hit it off with someone and agree to live together, great. But seriously, don't go into summer orientation with the expectation of finding your roommate. Your odds are just as good (if not better) for becoming well matched by being randomly assigned to someone. Having fun with a new friend for forty-eight hours does not mean they'll be a great roommate for you. Take it easy.

4. FINDING YOUR BEST FRIENDS.

Whether you are aware of it or not, deep down you are hoping to meet your best friends during these few days of summer orientation. Again, please absolve yourself of this expectation. The people you meet and hang with during this time will be lovely short-term friends, but it is extremely rare for people to end their college experience with their very best friends being the people they met during orientation. So, of course, be friendly. Get people's names and contact info. Connect with them on social media. But don't be discouraged if you feel lonely during these few days. Don't beat yourself up if you don't connect with anyone on a deep level. It takes lots of time to find your college besties. Do not worry about making this happen during orientation.

Enjoy it. Meet lots of people. Register for classes. Shake hands with one or two of your professors. Feeling really brave? Introduce yourself to the dean of your college or even the president of your university! Walk around and get to know your campus. Play a bunch of goofy icebreakers. But do your best not to stress about any of it. **Orientation is not an indicator of how well you'll do in college or what your experience will be like.** Take a deep breath, try to relax, and just have fun.

Should I Live with My High School Bestie?

Concern 2

> "My high school bestie and I both got into the same college, and I think we are going to live together. It seems like a no-brainer instead of each taking a random roommate who might be terrible. Don't you think?"

I want to tread lightly here, because I don't know you or your best friend personally, but I do know the many girls I have had this conversation with. And every time, without fail, I beg them not to live together.

No matter who your college roommate is, whether she's your lifelong best friend, a high school acquaintance, a girl you met at orientation, or a random assignment, it is going to be difficult. Many students heading off to college have never shared a bedroom, or sometimes even a bathroom, with another person. We just aren't used to having someone else in our personal space. And your dorm room is the *only* personal space you get in college, and it's shared! Now, those of you who shared a room with a sibling will typically do better than those of us who never did, but it is still a different ball game when living with a peer or friend than it is with a family member.

So first, just hear me say that having a roommate is going to be hard. It will challenge you and push you to die to self, to confront when necessary, to communicate in conflict, and to do so many other things. I wish I could sit down with you individually to talk about your specific situation, but here are some thoughts that I want you to consider.

I KNOW SHE'S YOUR BESTIE, BUT ARE YOU COMPATIBLE ROOMMATES?

Best friends don't always—and, actually, rarely—make the best roommates. Often what you want in a best friend is different from what you want in a compatible roommate. Roommate compatibility usually looks like someone who has the same values as you, someone who has the same level of cleanliness (or sloppiness) that you do, and someone who likes to go to bed and wake up around the same time as you.

If I had gone to the same college as my high school best friend, I'm sure we would have chosen to live together. After all, she was my bestie! But at that age, our ideas of cleanliness and our sleep schedules looked drastically different. She was a total night owl, and I liked to go to bed around 11 p.m., which meant our rising hours were very different. She also wasn't one to be bothered with things like making the bed or hanging up her clothes—she had better things to do. While I, on the other hand, became an extreme neat freak once being confined to a tiny dorm room. I needed everything in its proper place at all times.

I'd like to think we could have made it work, because we knew each other well and had similar values, but I can only imagine the tension that would have grown as a result of our incompatible sleep schedules and my desire for the room to be perfectly clean versus her free-spirited attitude about it all. One of us would have eventually resented the other, and things could have gone wrong fast, which leads me to my next question.

IF THINGS GO BAD IN THE RELATIONSHIP, IS THAT OKAY?

I have seen high school best friends completely ruin their relationship by living together. It happens all the time. I'm not trying to scare you out of living with your best friend, but you need to decide if it's worth the risk. You may not completely sever the relationship, but it is very, very possible your friendship will change due to living together. Sometimes the conflict is over compatibility issues; other times the conflict is over one of the roommates wanting more space and her own group of friends. Then the other roommate ends up getting her feelings hurt and a giant void grows between them. Soon they are strangers who barely speak to each other when in the room at the same time. Ouch!

IF YOU LIVE TOGETHER AND EVERYTHING IS MAGICAL, WILL YOU STILL MAKE FRIENDS ASIDE FROM EACH OTHER?

If there is a chance you will cling to each other and do everything together, I would strongly urge you to live with other people. Part of college is making new friends, branching out, becoming the best version of yourself. It's hard to do those things when you have your loyal sidekick attached to your hip 24/7. Better yet, you get to attend the same college as your best friend, and you can stay besties while living apart. You could live in the same dorm, or if you are just dying to be near each other, you could try to live in the same suite. But if you choose to live apart, you are giving each other room to breathe and widening your net to meet more people and have a larger community. I've seen roommates who are inseparable and share all the exact same friends. While it's great to share some of the same friends, it's also important to be individuals and do your own thing at times.

Over the years, I've witnessed several best-friends-turned-roommates who ended up ruining their friendships. It's horrible! Why not choose to live apart, knowing that it will put less pressure on your friendship and overall will be better for both of you? Yes, you could have an awfully weird roommate, but read on. Chapter Five is all about those crazies and how God uses them to make us grow and mature. It's all part of the journey!

Why Am I Fighting with My Parents All the Time?

Concern 3

> "I haven't even left for college yet, and it seems
> like all I do is fight with my parents."

For the most part, I had a really good relationship with my parents while growing up. Sure, we had occasional disagreements, but overall I really liked them and they really liked me...until my senior year of high school. Then everything changed. I felt like they were the enemy whose sole purpose was to prevent me from growing up, becoming independent, and doing what I wanted to do.

Sound familiar? If yes, let me shed some light on your situation.

In a sense, your biological clock is ticking—NOT the baby-making one (please), but the I-wanna-grow-up one. As the prospect of freedom and independence comes closer and closer, you are beginning to stretch your wings a bit more, perhaps pushing your limits a little further. You may also be choosing to spend more time around your friends than around your family. The desire to soak up the last few glorious months of high school with your besties far outweighs your desire to hang with your parental units and siblings.

Meanwhile, your parents are getting nervous, thinking, *Did we raise her well enough? Teach her everything she needs to know? Will she make good decisions? Will she manage her schedule well?* Their time raising you is coming to a close. They so badly want you to be successful in college, and part of them feels responsible for it—as if it will be their fault if you aren't. (By the way, it's 100 percent on you. You can go ahead and stop blaming your parents for ANYTHING in your life now. I'm serious.)

They may be tightening their grip on you. They are realizing this is the last few months they have with you before everything changes. They are sad, maybe even remorseful, that you will be moving out soon. Just like you want to soak up time with your friends, they want to soak up every last moment they have with you. When you choose to hang with your friends over them, it's like rubbing salt in their wounds. I'm not saying don't hang out with your friends and only spend time with your family. What I am saying is: **Give your parents some grace.**

Tensions are high because they want to hang on to you and have every last minute with you, while you are wanting the opposite. Be kind to Mom and Dad. Be sweet to your siblings. These people know you better and love you more than anyone else in the world. Don't be a jerk to them your last few months of living at home.

Consider this verse:

Children, obey your parents in the Lord, for this is right. "Honor your father and mother"—which is the first commandment with a promise—"so that it may go well with you and that you may enjoy long life on the earth." (Ephesians 6:1–3 NIV)

You may have heard this verse a hundred times, and it gets old fast, but it's a vital reminder. Don't just obey your parents; honor them. Also, I never cease to be amazed that this commandment came with a promise. If you honor your parents, it will go well with you. Somehow God designed this relationship to work so that by honoring your parents, you have a better and longer life. What's even crazier is that this verse doesn't say, "Children, obey your parents in the Lord and honor them *if they are good, loving, kind parents*." The command isn't conditional. It doesn't matter how your parents behave; you are supposed to obey and honor them.

Of course, God is our ultimate authority. So if our parents tell us to do something that is against God's Word, we obey God. You don't jump off a cliff if your parents tell you to, just like you don't give an alcoholic mother a drink because she says so. But within the moral reason of God's law, we are supposed to obey our parents and honor them, and we can honor our parents even amidst all of their frailties, brokenness, and sin.

Here's another verse to chew on:

> Be kind to one another, tenderhearted, forgiving one another, even as God in Christ forgave you. (Ephesians 4:32 NKJV)

Be kind to your family. Be kind to your parents, and don't forget your siblings! If this is a struggle for you, ask God to help you. You've got access to the fruit of the Spirit: love, joy, peace, patience, kindness, goodness, faithfulness, gentleness, and self-control (see Galatians 5:22–23). If you have placed your faith in Jesus, His Spirit dwells in you (see 1 Corinthians 3:16). Ask Him to pour those out of you when relating to your family.

Want to Take This to the Next Level?

Write your parents a handwritten card thanking them for specific ways they have provided for you and cared for you recently. Drop it in the mail or just leave it on their bed. They'll love it. I promise if you change your attitude toward them—giving them grace and seeing their perspective—it will lighten the tension. It will also help you grow! Life is full of difficult relationships, and some of God's greatest lessons for us are all about how well we deal with them. Practice now with those parental units, who, deep down, love you like crazy.

Freshman Year: The Number One Thing

Concern 4

> "What's the number one thing I should focus
> on for my first semester of college?"

I've received this question countless times over the years. It's the first semester of your freshman year, and everyone is trying to figure out the answer. What should be your top priority? What is the most important thing for you to do? How do you strive for success in college?

First, let me say this. I'm proud of you for thinking about this. It means you are striving to live life intentionally. You aren't just letting life happen to you. You are attempting to live with purpose and meaning. That is half the battle!

Now, there are a lot of plausible answers to this question. People will say you need to focus on time management, organization, eating/sleeping/exercising well, establishing a solid routine, concentrating on your studies and grades, fitting in socially on campus, getting involved, getting to know faculty, choosing your major...The list goes on and on. All of those are good answers. All are important.

But the number one thing I tell students to focus on their first semester is finding great friends. I realize this may not be the most popular answer with the parents—you go to college for academics, not a social life!—but friendship and community are a huge part of college and, I will argue, a huge part of life, which is why I want you to put some intentionality behind it as you create a new community of friends in college.

God actually created you and me with an innate need and desire for connection and relationship. He wired us to be a friend and want friends. So I will argue that your success and happiness in college will be directly impacted by the friends you choose. In fact, I'll say it even more boldly: **The friends you choose to surround yourself with will determine the course of your life.**

That may seem extreme, but it couldn't be more true. And I've watched this play out in both holistic and quite specific ways.

One of my past jobs was to prepare students for a career in the music industry. These were students majoring in music business, audio engineering, and the like. Year after year, I watched hundreds of students graduate from the program and either struggle to find a job or, after lots of applications and interviews, land a job they were pretty darn excited about.

One time, I ran into a former student who was complaining about being misled and unprepared by college for employment in the music industry. "Literally none of my friends have jobs!" he lamented. *Interesting,* I thought. *Yet I know dozens of alumni from your class who do.* And that's when I started noticing the trend in friend groups.

Nine times out of ten, I could look at a friend group from the music business program and see that either everyone in it had a job in the music industry or they were all still struggling to find work and complaining about how hard it was to get a professional job. Somehow the friends they surrounded themselves with had a direct impact on their postgraduation employment. While I haven't conducted any kind of official study, my theory is that the "successful" friend groups all encouraged and challenged one another throughout college to get great internships, attend networking events, and build meaningful relationships with professionals in the industry and even helped one another connect to folks in the industry. The other friend groups didn't do those things. Sure, they may have each interned once or twice, but they weren't the type of students who were working hard and putting in the effort to really advance in their desired field. So the friends they hung out with during college impacted the choices they made during their four years, which directly impacted their employment opportunities.

In a more holistic sense, we've all heard the old saying "You are who your friends are," and that statement is true! Your friends will rub off on you and will largely impact who you decide to be—what your character is like, what you value, and what you believe. So it is vital that you find people who share your values and who inspire, encourage, and positively challenge you. Choose friends who are the kind of people you want to be like. Surround yourself with a community that is going to make you a better person.

The hardest part about this is that it takes time and intentionality on your part. It means that the friends from your orientation group or your residence hall, though they are convenient friends, may not be the friends who fit the criteria.

Convenient friendships are rarely inspiring, meaningful friendships, because they are just that: convenient. Those people become your friends purely based on ease and proximity. Now, that doesn't mean they are bad friendships, but meaningful friendships require a lot more depth and purposeful connection. And I want meaningful friendships. In fact, I want to be an inspiring friend. Don't you?

But it takes time. It takes patience and pursuit. You will have to meet a lot of people. You'll have to observe them and determine if they are folks you want to be like, who share your values, who will encourage you. Then you'll have to pursue them and put in the time to develop a great friendship.

The other piece to this is that *you* have to be a great friend. You have to be a person whom others want to be like, whom others will find encouraging and inspiring. You can't look for great friends until you are ready to be one yourself.

Many sophomores come back to campus for their second year and realize the friendships they made last year are mediocre at best. If this is you, that's okay. Now you know and you've got three more years to find great friends. It's never too late!

Pursue meaningful relationships. Pursue friends you want to be like. Pursue friends who speak truth and show grace. Pursue friends who have a deeper walk with Jesus. Pursue friends who believe and trust God in far greater ways than you do. And don't stop with your peers! Find an adult on your college campus or in your church whom you want to be like as well. Find someone a few years ahead who can speak even more wisdom and truth into your life than a peer can. Look for adults who can guide you professionally, but also look for adults who can guide you personally. Who has a relationship with Jesus that you admire? Who has a marriage that you would like to emulate someday? Who is someone who seems to tackle life's obstacles with good sense and grace whom you can learn from?

You have to pursue great people. You begin this habit in college and, if you want to continue growing and living the richest life possible, you continue to pursue great people until the day you die. If you keep this a number one priority for your entire life, I promise it will be a rewarding one. When you pursue great friends, they will determine the course of your life, which will be greatness.

Gaining the Freshman Fifteen
Concern 5

"I'm so afraid I'm going to gain the freshman fifteen!"

It surprises me that this is still a thing, but I continue to hear girls talk about it all the time. A lot of research has been published attempting to debunk the myth of the freshman fifteen. Most studies show female college freshman tend to gain three or four pounds, not fifteen.[1] Whether it's fact or fiction, you don't need to be terrified of the freshman fifteen. It's as simple to keep it off as it is to put it on.

Watch out for these pitfalls:

BEER.
A lot of college students (men and women) gain weight due to excessive drinking. Think about it. An average beer is 150 calories. A glass of red or white wine is about 120 calories. Cocktails tend to fall between 120 and 200 calories but can be even more. For example, a piña colada is 490 calories![2] And that's a small serving, not the giant ones with umbrellas sticking out of them. Those calories add up really fast—especially if you are drinking in mass quantity several nights a week. Suddenly, you are pouring hundreds of extra calories into your body that it just isn't accustomed to processing.

JUNK FOOD, THE FOURTH MEAL.

Thanks to Taco Bell, we all know what the "fourth meal" is. Eating late-night junk food on a regular basis is another reason freshmen tend to gain weight. If your body isn't used to eating junk food, or if eating late at night is a new habit, this will certainly add on the pounds.

"I WALK A LOT."

If you were an athlete in high school or exercised regularly, you may experience a drop in physical activity when you get to college. I often hear, "But my campus is so big I walk a lot!" That is not the same amount of exercise or calorie burn as engaging in sports.[3] If you were really physically active in high school, you have to maintain the same level of activity if you expect your body to stay the same.

YOU'RE BECOMING A WOMAN.

Eye roll, I know. But it's true. The female body goes through its last stage of "girl to woman" when you hit college age. Whether it's during your freshman year or later on, you'll find your body weight shifting. For many of us, this means an extra five to ten pounds. Just embrace it. You're not a little girl anymore, and your body is making an adjustment. As I've said before, the way you live your life now is creating patterns and habits that are incredibly hard to break in your twenties and thirties. If you start freaking out over five pounds added to your frame today, I guarantee you will spend the rest of your life obsessed with every pound you add or subtract. Life is just too short for that, ladies. Yes, we should strive to be healthy people, but five pounds here or there is a waste of psychological, emotional, and physical energy. You have way more important things to be concerned about. Don't let five pounds steal your joy.

The general rule is if you maintain your eating and exercise habits from high school, you really should have no issues with keeping the freshman fifteen far away. However, if you are drinking excessively, eating way more junk food than you did previously, or exercising less, you will definitely see a change.

I'm Overwhelmed

Concern 6

"I am only a few days into my freshman year
and am feeling completely overwhelmed."

First of all, you are not alone. EVERYONE is feeling overwhelmed. It might look different on other people, but that's
based on how they are coping. Some withdraw, hide in their
rooms, and get very homesick and lonely. Others push into the
feeling and try to do everything, be everywhere, and become so
busy that they don't have a second to think about how overwhelmed they are. Others drink to make the feeling go away.
Others cope by studying a lot. The list of coping mechanisms is
endless, but you get the idea.

The point is that everyone feels overwhelmed and is just trying
to cope with it in different ways. I touched on this in Chapter Two,
but I find we all need to be reminded of the same truths many
times before they really sink in. Remember:

IT'S OKAY TO FEEL OVERWHELMED.

It's normal. Your lifestyle as you have known it for the past eighteen
years has been completely turned upside down, and you've been
given a lot of new decisions to make. *Which student organizations
do I want to be in? Should I join a sorority? Can I handle sixteen
credits? Whom do I want to spend time with? What friendships
should I pursue?* Meanwhile, you're trying to figure out if college
classes are more rigorous than high school and how to share a room

with someone else, and basically proving to yourself that you can do this. Of course you feel overwhelmed. Who wouldn't?

REMIND YOURSELF EVERY DAY: IT WILL GET BETTER.
You have to believe this. Trust me when I tell you: It gets better. Or find an upperclassman and let her tell you. It truly does get better, but you have to believe it in order to push through. Otherwise, you will drown in feeling overwhelmed. All you need to focus on right now is one day at a time.

SHARE WITH YOUR PEERS.
If everyone around you is pretending like they've got it together, that's how they're coping: pretending. Be the brave freshman who shares with her friends how she is really feeling, and bust into your community with some honesty. If you admit that things aren't easy, there will be a domino effect, and suddenly everyone around you will start to admit it too. There is strength in communities where people are vulnerable and truthful about how it's really going. Remember, you have the power to normalize other people's experiences by sharing. No one is alone!

FOCUS ON WHAT'S MOST IMPORTANT.
You are feeling overwhelmed because, frankly, there are just too many new things and new decisions for you to make. You have plenty of time to make all those decisions (which organizations, campus ministries, sorority, major, minor). Trust me on this. You can actually make all of those decisions I just listed your sophomore year. Some of you won't find your best fit on campus until your second or third year, so take the pressure off yourself now and decide what is most important to you. I would suggest making your top two priorities finding great friends and working hard in your classes. (Read Concern 4, "Freshman Year: The Number

One Thing," if you haven't already.) Identify what's most important and base your decisions on those things. Don't worry about
the rest; you have four whole years to do it all. This is just semester one of eight!

DON'T WORRY ABOUT ANYTHING...

> Don't worry about anything; instead, pray about everything.
> Tell God what you need, and thank him for all he has done.
> Then you will experience God's peace, which exceeds any-
> thing we can understand. His peace will guard your hearts
> and minds as you live in Christ Jesus. (Philippians 4:6–7
> NLT)

God's Word says, Don't worry about this! He's got this. Fight
your anxiety, fear, and overwhelmed feelings with prayer and a
thankful heart. Allow God to fill those anxious places with His
peace and a greater trust in Him. He's got this. You've got this. It
will get easier. I promise.

I Want to Reinvent Myself

Concern 7

A lot of us go to college with a plan to reinvent ourselves. It's not that I didn't like who I was in high school; in fact, I did like myself! I liked my friends and my reputation, but there was something so exciting and freeing when I imagined attending a university where no one knew me. I would get a clean slate. No one would be able to prejudge me based on something I did or didn't do in high school. The idea of completely starting over was so attractive I didn't even apply to any of the colleges in my state. I was determined to get away from everyone I had known so I was free to be exactly who I wanted to be.

Maybe that resonates with you, or maybe you're attending a college where you have a lot of high school friends but you'd still like to become a different version of yourself than you used to be. If you are thinking about reinventing yourself, here are a few questions I learned along the way that are worth considering.

1. ASK YOURSELF, *WHAT AM I RUNNING AWAY FROM?*

Like I said, when I went to college, I was ready for a clean slate. I was tired of being my father's daughter (the preacher's daughter of a large church) and just wanted to be known as Hanna No-Last-Name. I was also ready to leave behind a lot of the messes I had made (ex-boyfriends, girls I had a lot of conflict with—you get the idea . . .). I needed a fresh start. It's not wrong to want a fresh start. In fact, it's great to get do-overs! Everyone deserves a chance to be the best version of themselves, and sometimes that's hard to do when everyone around you knows all your past goof-ups and mistakes. But we still need to be cautious and evaluate our motives. What are you running away from? Name it. Identify it. Write out a multipage list if you need to. I've learned over the years that when I let things go unnamed in my life, they tend to have power over me. But if I can label it and call it like it is, there is freedom in pulling the skeletons out of the dark closet and into the light. Suddenly, they lose their power over me, and now I have the ability to do something about them.

So define what it is you are running away from. And then you need to ask yourself two follow-up questions. First, *Is this something I need to clean up before moving on?* As I mentioned, I was ready to get away from messes I had created. While I was able to run away from them my freshman year, guess where I ended up that following summer? At home with all those same people. It really wasn't until halfway through college that I decided to face the music and actually repair the high school friendships I had damaged. Not only did that do something really important for my heart—it's not healthy for you to go through life knowing you've hurt people and haven't attempted to make amends—but those high school friends ended up being part of my favorite summer in college. I'm so grateful to know that after all these years, even though I haven't spoken to some of those people in ages, I am in good standing with them. I can't imagine the regret I'd have today if I hadn't tried to make things right.

Second, ask yourself, *Is this something I'll regret leaving behind?* While I definitely wanted to run away from being the preacher's daughter, I didn't understand how important that piece of my identity was. Now, don't get me wrong, I don't go around introducing myself as a pastor's kid, but for better or worse, it's a huge part of why I am the way I am. Trying to leave that piece of me behind wasn't helpful in my growth into who God designed me to be. God chose for me to be born to a preacher man. I needed to learn how to appreciate and value that aspect of my upbringing in order to be the best version of myself. Maybe you're running away from a controlling mom or an annoying sister. Or perhaps you're fleeing from another form of identity, like I was with my PK label. Maybe you were a high-performing athlete who is sick and tired of being an athlete. Or perhaps you were the friend everyone called when they needed help, and you're tired of always giving and never getting. Whatever it may be, think through whether it's something you actually need to shed or something you just need to learn to repackage and hold in a different light as you move into college.

2. ASK YOURSELF, *WHAT AM I RUNNING TOWARD?*

So you want to reinvent yourself or at least become a better version of who you are? Great! Who is she? What is she like? Who are you going to be? In other words, what are you running toward? Does it align with your personal beliefs and values? Are you striving to be genuinely you, or are you striving to fit in as best you can? What do you want your reputation to be? What do you want people to say about you when you leave the room? Who does God want you to be? Who has He intentionally designed you to be? Do yourself a favor and identify who you think God wants you to be and what your values are. You can't just reinvent yourself blindly. You must do it with purpose. Again, write these things down. I can't stress enough how impactful it is for you to put pen to paper and identify these kinds of things. Even better, verbally process them with someone you trust. Share who you dream of being and ask them to share with you. Help each other strive to be the women God designed you to be.

3. ASK YOURSELF, *WHO AM I GOING TO SURROUND MYSELF WITH?*

I already said it in Concern 4, but at the end of the day, you are going to look a lot like the group of friends you choose. So if you want to reinvent yourself, you need to look for friends who are people you want to emulate. Choose friends who share the same values as you. Choose friends who have strong character. Choose friends who are loyal. If you just go along with the first group of friends you meet, I guarantee you will end up looking just like them and you probably won't like yourself. Most freshmen and sophomores who do this eventually walk away from their original college friend group and start their friend search process all over. And that's not a bad thing! There are worse things than realizing midcollege you don't really like your friend group. It's never too late to start over and find people who encourage you to be the best version of you.

So go for it. Run fast after who you believe God created you to be. You're getting a clean slate, and that's amazing. Just make sure you're being intentional and careful about who you are surrounding yourself with and, ultimately, who you are crafting yourself to be.

Should I Rush?

Concern 8

One of my only college regrets is not rushing. As a freshman, I went to the very first sorority recruitment event of the year. Hundreds of girls with name tags on their chests mixed and mingled on an outdoor terrace on a very hot August night in Nashville, Tennessee. I was terrified.

I wasn't, by any means, the most popular girl in high school, but I was known, liked, outgoing, and friendly. Overall, I was pretty darn self-confident in my high school surroundings. But being the new kid, a small fish in a big pond, and having to meet hundreds of new faces was not easy for me. I was scared, and while I may have put on a brave face, I had a lot of self-doubt amid the whole experience.

So after the first night of recruitment, I didn't go back. It was hard meeting all those new people, and I didn't like the idea of having to prove myself.

A year later, I transferred. I had the opportunity to start again at a new school, and my roommate (who was not new but who was also a sophomore) wanted to rush. She really wanted me to go with her, but I chickened out. Again.

If you had known me in high school, it would have seemed completely out of character that I would wimp out of something like sorority recruitment. But the truth was, I felt really out of my comfort zone and it terrified me. And that's why I regret not rushing. Not because I think I wrecked my college experience by not being in a sorority, but because I chose not to participate in sorority life simply out of fear.

Don't let fear of rush or anything else be the reason you miss out. Fear is a great thing to listen to when you're standing on the edge of a cliff that plummets down hundreds of feet to what would be a gruesome death. Fear, in those situations, keeps us safe from physical harm. And that's good! But a lot of times, fear gets in the way of us trying new things, taking risks, and, sometimes, experiencing greatness. Don't let a little fear or discomfort steal a great opportunity from you.

Now, if you can get over the idea that rush seems scary or weird, let's evaluate rushing and sorority life.

YOU CAN RUSH AND NOT PLEDGE.

I think the entire process of rushing is good for you. You will meet so many new people. You will be forced to learn how to socialize, network, ask questions, and talk about yourself—all things you never stop doing in life, and all things that are really important when it comes to professionalism, job searching, and your career. So what's the harm in trying it out? Go through the process and then decide if you actually want to pledge. There is nothing wrong with saying, "No, thanks," at the end of it all.

IT DOES COST MONEY.

The haters of Greek life will say, "You are paying for friends." If only it were that simple! Truthfully, you're paying for a lot of events, T-shirts, and other things, but you still have to put in the work to become friends with the gals in your sorority. Yes, it does cost money, and that price point differs widely based on the university you attend. You need to ask yourself realistically, *Can I afford sorority life?* Where you choose to spend your money is all about priorities, and whether you want to prioritize Greek life is totally up to you. However, this is partially a financial decision, and you need to consider that.

THERE ARE MAJOR COMMUNITY AND NETWORKING BENEFITS.

Some universities are hard to navigate without being part of a sorority. It is instant community, and that's not a bad thing. You do need to find your niche and your people somewhere. If that's in a sorority, great! If it's not, you just have to find it elsewhere, and that's great too! As you know, I didn't participate in sorority life, so I found my people primarily in Residence Life, a Christian organization, and the a cappella community. And it was wonderful.

Another positive to Greek life is the lifelong network it becomes. I have many friends who got their first job (or second or third) because of their sorority. It's a sisterhood that will open doors for you—even if it's just to get your foot in the door.

BUT WHAT ABOUT THE ALCOHOL ABUSE AND HAZING?

Every sorority and college is different. You are going to have to investigate what sororities are like at your school—and a great way to do that is through recruitment week! I personally know of several sororities where it's not a big deal if you don't drink. I also know of ones where it's impossible not to drink.

I had a friend in college who was a strong believer, someone who wasn't caught up in the partying scene but had a desire to be in a sorority, with the goal of becoming president her senior year. She wanted to be part of changing the culture of sorority life. She introduced spiritual elements into her sorority's meetings, offered optional Bible studies, and shifted the culture away from "get drunk" hazing to a strong sisterhood community based on deep friendships and common values. She genuinely changed her sorority from the inside out. I'm not saying you have to do that, but I am saying it's an option. If Greek life is really dark on your campus and you feel called to join it to be a light in the darkness, go for it! Just make sure you have some great Christian friends somewhere on campus who will surround you, support you, and help you keep being a light.

Overall, I think a strong first step is to try out recruitment and see how it goes. You'll learn more about the sororities at your school instead of stereotyping them, and you won't let a little fear or discomfort prevent you from trying something that could be great!

I'm Just Not Happy Here
Concern 9

> "Everyone says that college is the best four years of your life, but so far it's been pretty hard and lonely. Why does it seem like everyone else is doing so much better than me? I'm wondering if I picked the wrong school and maybe need to transfer."

Listen to me. YOU ARE NOT ALONE. A lot of students feel this way. As I mentioned in Chapter One, it's a huge pet peeve of mine when people say that college is the best four years of your life. Why? Because it sets you up for ridiculously high and, in my opinion, false expectations. Yes, college is amazing. You get to taste freedom and independence with very little responsibility. You get to be involved in things that grow and excite you. You are surrounded by community and friends you can hang with at any hour of the day. All of those things are great, but it doesn't mean that college comes without hardship, without challenges, or without times of feeling lonely or discouraged.

So if you're feeling like college has been a bit of a letdown, you are not alone. You have not failed. It's a common feeling.

Now, first things first. If you are a freshman or transfer student feeling this way, I need to remind you that you haven't been at school for very long. Seriously. Take a minute to look at your calendar and add up the number of weeks you've been at your college. I know it feels like you've been there awhile, but it really hasn't been that long. Think about your best friends from home. How long did it take for you to build those friendships? I'd bet a lot of money that it took way more time than just a few months. Anytime you move and have to cultivate new friendships, it takes time. In my personal life, each time I moved, it took me about a year to start making a new place really feel like home.

YOU NEED TO GIVE YOURSELF SOME GRACE AND SOME MORE TIME, AND BE PATIENT WITH THE PROCESS.

No matter where you are in the semester or year, you still have more time. I promise that if you put in the effort, you will know more people and have better friendships at the end of the semester than you do today. However, you may still leave school for the winter or summer break and not really want to go back. That's okay. That's normal too.

While I liked my first semester of college, I also would have been just fine staying home after winter break. Nothing made me excited about going back to school. Again, that is totally normal— just don't let it prevent you from going back this early in the game!

You may finish your entire freshman year, go home for the summer, and still not be pumped about going back to school. Is that normal? Yes! Is that everyone's experience? No, but let me say it again: For being at college for only nine months, it's okay if it doesn't feel like home yet or you still don't have a deep sense of belonging or community. Remember, these things take time.

NOW, A NOTE ABOUT COMPARING YOURSELF TO OTHERS.

You may be thinking, *It seems like everyone else is doing so much better than me.* Sure. For some people change, transition, making new friends, and making a new home come easier. But not everyone is over the moon about their college experience. A lot of people are faking it till they make it. Don't be afraid to ask others how they are really doing. They may be struggling just as much as you are but are afraid to admit it. Most people who feel this way also feel like they are the only ones who feel this way. You can be the person who is honest with others about how the college transition has been for you. I think you'll be surprised at how many others agree it's been tough, once they hear you share.

One final comment about transferring. The college girl who was quoted at the beginning of Concern 9 mentioned transferring. Please, I beg you, don't transfer until you've been at college for a full year. Please don't transfer after one semester. Living in a place for three and a half months is not enough time to judge it and jump ship. Give your college campus a full year, then reassess. As I mentioned earlier, I was a transfer student, and it was absolutely the right decision for me. But I transferred due to financial reasons, wanting to be closer to home, and changing my major, not because my first semester wasn't as amazing as everyone said it would be.

It will get better. I promise. But it takes time and effort.

But Should I Transfer?

So you've read Concern 9, have given yourself time (at least more than one semester!), and still wonder if there is a better college fit out there for you. It's time for a good old-fashioned reflection assignment:

Find a corner in your favorite spot on campus and write out your answers to the following questions. Actually write them. It doesn't matter if you type them out on your computer or write them by hand in a spiral-bound journal, but you need to write it down. There is something so much more clarifying when you can see something on paper versus when it's all in your head. So write them down. They doesn't have to be full sentences; bullet points will do!

1. Why do you want to transfer? What is lacking at your school?

Be honest. Write down everything, big and small, that you can think of. From lack of friendships to the weather, bad food at the cafeteria, whatever! Every complaint you can muster up, write it down.

2. What are the good things you'll miss (if you do transfer)?

Don't just write "friends"; write down every name that comes to mind of someone you'll miss. Don't just write "scholarship money"; add up the total dollar amount you'll be giving up and write that down. Be specific.

3. What's better where you're considering going?

If you don't have at least one other school you're contemplating, then you're not really serious about transferring. Stick with where you are, or spend some time researching alternative options soon. If you are juggling a few different options, answer this question for each school you are considering.

Or perhaps you're not considering transferring to another school but, instead, moving back home for a year or taking some other kind of gap year. Whatever the alternate plan may be, write down all of the pros for this option that you can think of.

4. What are the potential challenges you'll face at the new school?

Of course, we don't know all the challenges that will come our way, but there should be at least a few things you can identify as cons to transferring to a new place.

Whether we're transferring schools or changing roommates, at some level, we're always trading a set of known problems for a set of unknown problems. That doesn't always mean the safest bet is to stay with our set of known problems. Many times change is worth the risk, but it's always of value to consider all the angles before making the trade.

As I said before, I transferred and it was absolutely the right decision for me to make, but only you can make this decision for yourself. Answer the previous questions and really take time to look over everything you write down. Consider the options. Pray over your lists. Ask God to give you wisdom and discernment. He promises in James He will always give wisdom to those who ask:

> If you need wisdom, ask our generous God, and he will give it to you. He will not rebuke you for asking. (James 1:5 NLT)

It's great to ask wise counsel of people whom you look up to, who live a life you respect, who are more mature than you. But again, only you can make this decision. After all, you are the one who has to live with the results!

How Much Should I Be Talking to Mom and Dad?

Concern 10

"It's been so hard being at college without my mom! She is truly my best friend and I'm having a difficult time not seeing her every day."

"My parents are driving me crazy. My mom or dad literally call every day and want to hear every detail of my life. Helloooo! I went to college out of state for a reason!"

You may not actually be thinking about this, but it's worth considering for a moment, and I want to address both extremes.

EXTREME 1: YOU TALK TO MOM EVERY HOUR OF EVERY DAY.

I get it. Your mom is your best friend. You are her only child, or maybe you're her favorite child. (Let's be real. Parents may say there is no such thing as a favorite child, but we all know the truth: They have favorites!) Even when you were in high school, you two texted throughout the day, every day. Now that you're in college, it's no different.

First, let me start by saying, I do not have a problem with you being best friends with your mom (or dad), or even texting them every day. What I want you to be cautious about is: Are you spending more time on the phone with Mom than with the people around you at college?

You wake up in the morning and text, "Morning, Momma! I'm

up!" You call her on your way to your first class. You call her on your way to class number two. You text with her through the majority of your lunch. You text her while studying. You call her again at night on your way to dinner. You call her at night for help on your paper.

Do you see where I'm going? You need to disconnect a bit from your momma and spend more time talking face-to-face with the people around you: your roommate, your classmates, your professors, your friends. There is a reason we say "go off" to college—even if it's in your hometown! Part of college is learning to detach a little from your parents and start growing into the independent adult God created you to be.

You are also missing out on the people and experiences around you if you spend more time on the phone with Mom than with anyone else on campus. Think about what you want to get out of college. When the four years are over and done, what do you want to look back on? What do you want to remember? What experiences do you want to have had? What words do you want to use to describe your time? Then think about what you need to start doing today in order to get there. May I kindly suggest maybe letting go a little from your umbilical-phone-cord attachment to Mom and instead trying to create meaningful connections to the people around you?

EXTREME 2: YOU FORGET ABOUT YOUR PARENTS ALTOGETHER.

Maybe you weren't super close with your parents, or you love them and have a great relationship but never shared a ton of details about your life. It can be easy to go weeks without contacting Mom or Dad—though usually one of them will pester you every once in a while just to make sure you're alive.

I highly encourage you to start taking an active role in developing an adult relationship with your parents. You are transitioning from a kid to an adult. Part of becoming an adult is learning how to have a mature friend-like relationship with Mom and Dad. Consider setting aside a time, just once a week, that you call your parents to update them on your time at college and to ask them about their life! I also highly encourage you to make sure you connect with both of them, if that's possible.

I had a bad habit of calling home just to talk to my mom. Even if my dad picked up, I'd say, "Hey, Dad. How are you?" ("Good.") "Can I talk to Mom?" And like the loving father he is, he'd pass the phone off and get the details of my life from her after we hung up. Little did I know, I was hurting his feelings! My dad wanted to hear from me. He wanted to have a direct relationship with me. It took one of his best friends calling me up to tell me that. I was practically heartbroken when I realized what I had been doing. I wasn't intentionally avoiding him. I was just used to sharing more details about my life with my mom. So when I went off to college, I sort of, accidentally, cut him out of my life.

All of that is to say, pursue your parents. Call them to connect and show you care about their lives as well!

A FINAL NOTE: IF YOUR MOM CALLS YOU 24/7 AND IS DRIVING YOU CRAZY...

Instead of ignoring her calls and texts and hurting her feelings, set a day/time with her when you promise to call. If you can say, "Hey, Mom. Sorry I'm not very responsive via text (or I can't answer when you call). I'll still do my best to respond, but how about we agree that I'll call you every Sunday at two p.m. and we can catch up on the week?" If your mom is trying to reach you all the time, she just misses you and wants to connect. So how happy will that make her if you initiate and show that you also want to connect regularly? That's all she wants. Of course, you have to actually follow through and do it. So set a reminder on your phone and just know you have a standing date with Mom. She will adore you for it.

How Do I Survive the Holiday Breaks at Home?

Concern 11

> "I am dreading going home for the holidays. My parents get all up in my details and even want me to have a curfew! I've gotten used to my college freedom. How do I reenter my family's world without losing my mind?"

Before you know it, you'll be heading home for winter break. But whether it's your first or fourth winter break, reentry to home life can always be a bit challenging. So let's talk about why your parents are driving you crazy.

THERE IS TENSION EVERY TIME YOU MAKE PLANS WITH FRIENDS INSTEAD OF HANGING OUT WITH THE FAMILY.

This was my number one problem when I was home from college. I would make plans as much as possible to see all of my high school friends. I wanted to soak up the time I had with them, since we didn't go to the same college. The problem was that this really hurt my parents' feelings. They wanted me to stay home for dinner and watch a movie with them at night.

Your parents have really missed you, and they want you around as much as possible. So when you prioritize plans with your friends, it might upset them. I'm not saying you can't hang out with your friends, but make sure you are carving out some family time and being intentional about making your parents (and siblings) feel like you want to be with them too.

YOUR PARENTS WANT TO KNOW THE WHO/WHAT/WHEN/WHERE OF ALL YOUR PLANS AND ARE MANDATING A CURFEW.

GASP. HOW COULD THEY BE SO RIDICULOUS?! Don't hate me when I say this, but you need to get over yourself. Your parents are used to being your parents—in other words, your protectors. They feel responsible for you, and the way they protect and care for you is by mandating a curfew and wanting to know all the details about your plans. I know you don't have to do this when you're at college, but you are back home right now, living under your parents' roof. You've got to suck it up and respect whatever rules they place on you. Seriously, it's just for a few weeks. Be kind, and honor Mom and Dad by abiding by their rules.

THEY ARE "HARASSING" YOU ABOUT YOUR LIFE PLANS—PRESSURING YOU ABOUT DECLARING YOUR MAJOR, STUDYING ABROAD, APPLYING FOR GRADUATE SCHOOLS, STARTING YOUR JOB SEARCH, AND MORE.

I remember several of my students struggling with this. It seemed like whenever they were home, it became a war zone: Mom and Dad versus the student, fighting over "the best plan." I knew a student who was a finance major because her dad said it was the only major he'd pay for. In reality, she desperately wanted to major in dance. She was miserable. Every time she went home, it was a constant battle with her dad, trying to convince him to let her change her major. If you are experiencing something similar, I encourage you to set some boundaries with your parents.

Don't let the *What are you going to do with your life?* topic pervade your entire break. When the topic comes up, say, "I want to talk about this, but I don't want this to be the only thing we discuss when I'm home. Let's talk about this over dinner tomorrow night." Then stick to it. When it is time to talk, hear them out.

It's vital that your parents feel like you are listening and taking in what they are saying. Then calmly and maturely state your case. Be an adult during this conversation. It's crucial that you don't act like the twelve-year-old kid your parents remember all too well. Finally, whether or not the topic is resolved, communicate boundaries again. Maybe say, "I understand we may need to talk about this more, but I don't want my time at home to be all about arguing over my plans. I want us to enjoy this time together. What can we do to accomplish that?" I know that may seem overly formal or professional, but you've got to communicate directly and maturely with your parents in order for them to respect you. They will always see you as their child, someone who needs their help and guidance, until you prove to them over and over again, for many years, that you are a responsible and trustworthy adult. This takes a lot of time. So be patient with them and be patient with the process. Patience, after all, is a mature quality that a twelve-year-old rarely possesses.

Bottom line: I know your parents may be driving you crazy for a variety of reasons, but be kind, mature, and respectful, and show them that you love them and care about them. This is much more about you changing your attitude and response to them than you trying to get them to treat you differently.

Six Steps for a Successful Reentry

1. Understand where your parents are coming from.

Your parents love you dearly and, therefore, feel responsible for you and your safety. While they didn't know where you were most of the time while you were off at college, things are different now. You are living at home under their roof again. They feel responsible. This is not their attempt to take away your newly found independence. This is their natural reaction of wanting to take care of you while you live in their home again. Remind yourself of this when they start drilling you with twenty questions on your plans for the evening or they get upset because you didn't come home for dinner.

2. Communicate with your parents.

Sit down over dinner when you first get home and ask your parents what their expectations are of you now that you are back at home. Do they expect you to be home by your high school curfew? Do they expect you to text them your whereabouts throughout the day? Do they expect you to help out with chores, chauffeuring your siblings around, or anything else? Here's the part you're not going to like: You have to say yes to their expectations. If they want you home by midnight every night, you have to do it. Why? Because they are your parents and you are living under their roof. If you don't want to comply with their expectations, pay rent and live somewhere else for the summer. No, I'm not kidding. Respect them and serve them when you're at home. That's your job as a child, even when you're a fifty-five-year-old child—you respect and serve your parents.

3. Be kind to your parents.

My parents didn't give me a curfew once I was home from college. However, my mom wouldn't go to bed until I was home. No matter what time it was, I would find her (well, okay, she was asleep, but...) on the couch in the living room. Out of guilt, I would always shoot to be home by

2 a.m. for her sake, but I wish I had come home sooner. Making your mom sleep on the couch until 2 a.m. isn't kind. I wish I had been kinder. What did I gain in those couple of hours every night over those winter and summer breaks? I couldn't tell you one memory from those nights, couldn't even tell you who I was hanging out with. Today, I look at my mom and think what a gift she is to me. She has served me her whole life. I could have come home earlier and let her have a full night's sleep in her own bed. Seems like an insignificant sacrifice in hindsight.

4. Consider your siblings.

If you aren't the oldest child, you'll understand this more easily. When you left for college, your younger sibling's life changed. She or he became the oldest child and has operated that way in your home for the past year. You are completely ruffling his or her feathers by coming home. While it's not your fault, just keep this in mind and be considerate. You could even—gasp—have a conversation with your siblings about your reentry. What if you asked them, "Now that I'm home for the break, what are things you're worried will change? How can I help? Are there things you wish I would do while I'm back home?" They may not have the maturity yet to answer your questions, but you can model the way and show them what it looks like to become a caring, servant-hearted adult—or at least a big sister!

5. Prioritize family time.

It's really easy to get swept away in hanging out only with your high school friends when you're home for the summer. And when your family gets ignored, it hurts their feelings. They may never say that, but it will show up in greater tension between you and them. Believe me. I've lived it. So prioritize spending time with Mom, Dad, and the sibs. Show them that they are important to you and that you value time with them too. Similarly, pitch in while you're at home. You're not around during the school year to help around the house, but that doesn't mean you no longer should. Do the dishes. Drive little Johnny to practice. Take Sarah to the pool. Help with the laundry. Want to do something crazy? Cook a meal for your family once a week while you're home. I dare you. Don't know how to cook? Ask your mom or dad to teach you while you're home. They won't know what to do with themselves!

6. During the summer, get a job or internship, or volunteer.

Don't you dare spend all summer just hanging out. If possible, make some money and save it for the school year! If not, at least get an internship or volunteer somewhere on a regular basis (ten hours a week or more). Think of it as a résumé builder and a way for you to be "others-focused" instead of being all about you. (Remember Chapter Three?) This will keep you from boredom, help you manage your time better, make you appreciate your time at home and with friends, improve your summer, and prevent your parents from viewing you as an entitled sloth. Win/win.

CHAPTER FIVE

Roommate Woes

College Girl Concerns 12–22

> I want to kill my roommate but don't know where to bury her body.
>
> —Anonymous

Maybe that exact thought has crossed your mind in recent months. If you can introduce me to a college girl who never had a roommate conflict all four years, I'll give you a crisp Benjamin Franklin. Whether you live with your best friend or a complete stranger, the likelihood that you will have conflicts is somewhere around 100 percent.

I know roommate conflicts are about the most frustrating thing on the planet. You want your home or dorm room to be a safe place where you can relax, unwind, and do your thing. When you and a roommate aren't getting along, it ruins that safe place and often unnerves you to your core. When home isn't a safe place for me to lay my head, I find that my heart has a similar problem resting. Here's the good news: Roommate conflicts are opportunities for growth. They are challenges you get to rise up and meet. They are situations perfectly crafted for you to learn how to communicate in conflict and, ultimately, become a better person. In fact, my dad used to always say to me, "Roommates are the best preparation you'll ever have for marriage." And you know what? It's true! Learning to live with someone else and how to compromise, sacrifice, confront behavior, and apologize when you're wrong is the best practice for marriage. So whether you want to be married someday or you just want to be a great human being, let's look at roommate conflicts as free opportunities to practice becoming the best version of you possible.

Communicating in Conflict

Concern 12

> "I need to confront a friend on some things that have happened recently, but I hate conflict! Any advice on how to best go into the conversation?"

Think about the last time you talked through a conflict with someone. Could be your mom or dad, boyfriend, best friend, roommate, classmate—you know, those pesky group projects. You get the idea.

Hopefully, this isn't hard for you to pinpoint. We experience conflict all the time if we are interacting with other human beings, but many times we don't choose to engage in the conflict. We brush it under the rug and hope it goes away. The hard truth is that we need to communicate in conflict. The primary reason roommate relationships are so difficult is because we don't communicate well with one another. We don't engage well in our conflicts.

Consider this question: What's your goal when you choose to communicate in conflict? You have a conflict with someone in your life, and it's bothered you so much you decide you have to address it. So while taking a shower or fixing your hair in the mirror, you practice what you're going to say, and you're ready. You've prepared your little speech. But what is your ultimate goal in this confrontation?

If I'm totally honest, my goal is to be heard. I want the other person to know what I am thinking or why I am feeling a certain way. If I can be even more brutally honest with you, I must confess that I think I am right 95 percent of the time. So when communicating in conflict, I think that if I can just express my opinion well enough to you, you will see that I am right, you'll agree with me, and our conflict will be over. How horrible is that? Not only is that incredibly selfish and self-centered, it is also an awful way to approach communicating in conflict. Proverbs 18:2 says, "A fool takes no pleasure in understanding, but only in expressing his opinion" (ESV).

So when I am only interested in expressing my opinion, well, the Bible doesn't mince words, does it? It says I'm behaving like a fool!

The goal of communicating in conflict should be mutual understanding and reconciliation. Mutual understanding means that first, I listen to you. I listen to you in such a way that I don't just hear you, but I try to understand you. I put myself in your shoes and imagine where you're coming from. I empathize. Then, hopefully, because I've done a good job understanding and empathizing, you do the same. You listen to me. You try to understand my point of view. You empathize with my feelings. Then, and only then, can we experience true reconciliation. I apologize for what I need to own, you do the same, and we both extend forgiveness and grace to each other.

Can a roommate conflict end in mutual understanding and reconciliation? Absolutely, but to pull it off, it takes two mature people who want to love God and others before themselves. So it's rare! But that shouldn't stop you from behaving the way you know God wants you to treat your roommate. Regardless of how you think your roommate will respond, the next time you choose to engage in conflict and communicate with her, be intentional about hearing her first. Make your goal to understand where she is coming from and what she is feeling. Remember, a "fool takes no pleasure in understanding, but only in expressing his opinion," and you, my friend, are no fool. So we must be wise and approach conflict with the intent to listen and understand.

If you begin with the goal of understanding your roommate, no matter what the situation may be, you will approach her with less anger, she will be less defensive, and there will be a greater probability that your conversation will have positive results. You can't control her or her response, but you can control yourself. Ultimately, you are accountable to God for your actions, but if He wants you to love your neighbor, it doesn't get much closer to home than your roomie.

Help—I'm Living with a Stranger!

Concern 13

> "I was randomly assigned a roommate, and now I'm a nervous wreck thinking about living with someone I've never met before. Help!"

Oh yes, the random roommate assignment. I love it so much! It fills my heart with joy thinking about all the eighteen-year-olds in the country who are about to be thrown into a living space, often smaller than the bedroom they grew up in, with a complete stranger for nine whole months. It's one of the best things on the planet, and it makes me giddy.

Why? Because it's so countercultural. In a society where we are all about "me," having it my way, and being as comfortable as possible, living with a random college roommate challenges all of those norms. I think that's amazing.

First, let me say if you are living with a random roommate assignment, I'm really proud of you. I think you are awesome for signing up to live with someone you've never met before. Even if you didn't have any other option but to go random, I'm still proud of you. Go ahead—pat yourself on the back. Maybe treat yourself to an ice cream cone or a pedicure. You deserve it.

If you are reading this prior to move-in day, here are five things about your new roomie I urge you to consider:

1. DON'T JUDGE HER BY HER SOCIAL MEDIA ACCOUNTS.

Seriously. Don't do it. I used to work in Residence Life, and I would get calls from incoming freshmen saying, "I can't live with this person!"

"You already know them?" I would ask.

"Well, no, we've never communicated, but I saw blah, blah, blah on her Facebook page, and I just can't live with someone like that!"

I know that sounds ridiculous, but it happens all the time. So don't do it. If you want to scope her out via social media, fine, but don't judge her. You probably don't want someone to judge you based on everything you post either. Social media doesn't give a complete picture of who a person is. In fact, it's only a very small window into someone's life and it's far too easy to jump to conclusions and misjudge or misunderstand that person entirely.

2. COMMUNICATE WITH HER THIS SUMMER, BUT DON'T OVERCOMMUNICATE.

Don't try to become best friends over text and Snapchat. Just erase that expectation from your mind. You'll have all year to get to know each other. Instead, be present where you are, with your family and friends from home. I have met random roommates who show up at college acting like they're best friends. One of the girls told me that she and her new roommate talked on the phone for hours each week leading up to move-in day. You know how that turned out? Not well. They set the bar too high on their relationship, and it ended up causing disappointment and hurt feelings. It's great to be friends with your roommate—heck, you can even be best friends—but you also have to have friends besides your roommate. Don't put all your eggs in one basket, so to speak. Don't spend tons of time over the summer trying to become besties with this new girl. You'll get to know each other very quickly once you move in together. It's all part of the process!

3. DO COMMUNICATE ABOUT MAJOR DORM ROOM ITEMS.

Do you want to have a TV in your room? A coffee maker? A mini fridge or microwave (if your room doesn't come with one)? A hot pot? Think about large items or appliances that you don't need duplicates of. Try to keep it fair on who provides what. I don't recommend splitting the cost of items. You buy things and bring them, and she can do the same, but when you split the cost it tends to become an issue when it's time to move out. Keep it simple by individually owning but sharing things.

4. DON'T WORRY ABOUT COORDINATING YOUR BEDSPREADS, WALL ART, ETC.

I've seen girls spend thousands—yes, thousands—of dollars on decorating their dorm room. Please, it's not worth it. The room will look great even if your sides don't match at all; I promise. You can also agree on waiting to buy things together once you both move in. For example, choose a floor rug together. But again, I don't recommend splitting the cost of things unless you both are okay with donating the rug to the trash bin once the school year is over. (And you may just want to do that, because unless you buy a vacuum, it may never get cleaned!)

5. GO IN WITH THE EXPECTATION OF LEARNING HOW TO BE A GREAT ROOMMATE, NOT MAKING HER YOUR BEST FRIEND.

Some of you will actually become best friends, and it's so fun when that does happen. But the majority of us live with roommates we wouldn't normally be friends with. The goal becomes learning how to live well with someone who is so different from you. It is one of the best character-building lessons you will ever experience.

My freshman year, I lived with a girl who could not have been more opposite to me. I learned so much about myself, how to communicate honestly and openly, how to stand up for myself, and how to let go of my-way-or-the-highway tendencies. I wouldn't trade that year for the world. Whether you become best friends or worst enemies (but let's not become worst enemies, yeah?), I promise it will be one of the most transformative experiences you encounter in the next four years.

Dirty Dishes, Stolen Food, and Other Things That Drive You Crazy

Concern 14

To say my roommate and I were opposites is an understatement. She was a hippie, a pot-smoking, free-loving, nonshaving kind of a girl. I was, well, none of those things. She was also extremely messy. I, of course, was a neat freak. We were both very kind and cordial to each other, but there was an invisible line down the middle of our room—her space and my space. I didn't want her to touch my things, and I definitely didn't want to touch any of her things! Shannon was the kind of girl who never cleaned a dish, washed her bedsheets, or sanitized anything (including herself) the entire year. She would order takeout but eat the food on reusable dishes, and everything would pile up around her bed and desk and on the floor. Within a few days, smells started to take over our room, and living organisms began to grow. It was bad.

I don't know what your roommate does that drives you crazy. Maybe she eats all your food, never offers to buy toilet paper, or can't shut a cabinet door to save her life. No matter what she does that makes your hair stand on end, you have a combination of three choices: Confront her, get over it, or let it drive you absolutely bananas.

I chose a combo of the first and last. I would constantly confront Shannon on the green fuzz and special odors that grew on her side of the room. Remember, we were kind to each other. So I said it sweetly and she responded understandingly, but nothing ever changed. Then, every day I would walk into the room and feel steam pouring out of my ears because I was so angry over her uncleanliness. Occasionally, this would come out in some kind of passive-aggressive act toward her, but mostly I just stuffed it down.

Here's the thing I didn't understand at the time: I can only control myself. No matter how hard I try, how persuasive, kind, or mean I am, I cannot control someone else's behavior. However, I can control myself.

If your roommate is driving you batty, I absolutely think you should talk to her about it. She may have no idea her bad habit is your greatest pet peeve. You do need to be kind and considerate in the way you explain it (read Concern 12 in this chapter if you haven't already), but I think confrontation and honest communication are really important and positive things! However, the bleak reality is, even if you have a great conversation, your roommate may not change at all. She may do just what Shannon did—nod, sympathize, apologize, promise to be cleaner, and then do absolutely nothing.

And that's when you have a choice to control yourself. You have the choice to get over it or to let it drive you absolutely insane.

"But, Hanna, *she* is *making* me insane!" you plead.

Actually, she's not. Remember, she can't control you. She can only control herself, and you can control yourself. You have the ultimate power in deciding how you will react to her bad habits.

I learned this when I was much older, postcollege, when I had roommates who could not—for the love!—put their dirty dishes in the dishwasher. They always left them in the sink. (Can you tell I'm a bit of a neat freak?) It drove me crazy. How freaking hard is it to move the dirty dish two feet from the sink to the dishwasher?

I was complaining to a friend one day, and she laughed out loud. "You are letting a silly dirty dish completely steal your joy!"

She was right. Something that doesn't matter at all, a dirty dish, was *killing* my mood. I may have had the best day at work, but walk into my house to find a dirty dish in the sink and suddenly my face is turning fifty shades of red. My great mood from my wonderful day is wrecked, thanks to a dirty dish! That may seem ridiculous to you (I mean, it *is* ridiculous), but think about it. Are you letting your roommate's bad habit impact you? Is it ruining your attitude or even your day? Is it stealing your joy?

That's when I realized I had a choice. I could pick up the dirty dish, put it in the dishwasher, and get over it. It's that easy. By simply putting the dish away, I have solved the problem. Now, I can't put the dish away and huff and puff about it. Nor can I get angry the next time it happens. I see the dish and make a concerted effort to think, "Ah! That's my job! I will put that dirty dish in the dishwasher! I love doing that!" I'm not being sassy or sarcastic. I'm choosing to have a positive attitude and I remove the problem.

"But, Hanna," you argue, "you shouldn't clean up after your roommate. You're just enabling her bad habits!"

You're right. While I agree with that statement, the bigger problem here, even bigger than enabling her bad habit, is that a dirty dish is stealing my joy. Yes, I could make it my mission to teach my roommate how to put her dishes in the dishwasher, and I'd probably never succeed, and I'd likely be angry and annoyed on a daily basis. Or I could solve my problem and stop allowing a dirty dish to steal my joy.

So what are you going to do? Let your roommate's habit drive you mad, or remove the problem and let it go? I guarantee that whatever she does, it isn't worth letting it steal your joy. Talk to her about it, absolutely, but then focus on controlling yourself. Like I've said before, this will make you a much better spouse and human being in the long run. Think of it as character-building and let it go!

She's Drunk and Loud, and I'm Just Over Here Trying to Sleep!
Concern 15

> "My roommate is constantly waking me up in the middle of the night because she comes home drunk. She is loud and obnoxious and totally oblivious that I am already in bed asleep!"

This one is a classic. For those of you in a similar situation, I'll let my friend tell more of her story, because I think you will connect:

> "I am a freshman in college and am already having a hard time with the adjustment. I am not a partier or a drinker, but my roommate and suitemates are. I've had a couple bad experiences and I'm contemplating moving out. But I really don't want to be that girl where when the going gets tough, I move out. I like my roommate a lot but am finding it very hard to live with her. She comes home drunk and turns the lights on in our room in the middle of the night and then the next morning acts like everything is fine. I try to talk to her about it, but I can never find the right words to say. Should I move out or stick with it?"

First of all, I love the silver lining in my friend's note. She likes her roommate a lot! That is already a huge win. Sometimes there are people we really like, people who are great friends, but who at the same time aren't compatible roommates. The good news is, it's a lot easier to compromise with someone you like. If you're in a similar situation, hang on to that. When you get in moments where your roommate annoys or frustrates you, remind yourself that *you like her*.

Now, to get down to business, you have to sit down and have a heart-to-heart with your roommate. Far too often, girls decide to move out of their living situation before ever trying to discuss with their roommate the things that are bothering them. That is not okay! You cannot go through life simply removing yourself from situations you don't like, and you shouldn't do that when it comes to your living situation either. Remember, roommate conflicts are an invitation for us to grow up, mature, learn to communicate, and ultimately become more like Jesus. I know, deep down, you want to do those things, so here's what you're going to have to do.

1. YOU HAVE TO TALK TO HER.

I know it seems scary or awkward, but you have to have a conversation with her about this—probably a few conversations—before it's okay to call it quits. Don't move out unless you've communicated your issues and have given her ample opportunity to come to a resolution. Bring it up in an easy, casual way. The next time you're both hanging out in your room (and no one else is there), just say, "Hey—I've been wanting to talk to you about something. Is now an okay time?" This is going to signal to her that what you have to say is important to you, but it's also not dramatic. Start by acknowledging how it may affect her and then explain how it affects you. "I know when you come home late at night, it's probably difficult, since I'm already asleep and all of the lights are off, but it stinks for me because . . . [it wakes me up, I can't go back to sleep, etc.]. Is there some way we can compromise?" That is the key ingredient. I know you may be thinking, *But, Hanna! Compromise?! She's stumbling home drunk and waking me from my beauty sleep! What is there to compromise about?!* Read on.

2. YOU'RE GOING TO HAVE TO COMPROMISE.

I know you might think I'm crazy for saying you need to ask for a compromise, but that's the only real resolution to this situation. You can't expect her to come home and get ready for bed in complete darkness (especially, unfortunately, if she's drunk). Nor can you demand she be home and in bed at the same time you are. It's her room too, after all. You two may need to buy a dim lamp she can use or think of another way she can get ready for bed without totally disturbing you. You may need to buy earplugs or an eye mask. I know that may seem unjust—why should you suffer, when she is the one coming home drunk and being inconsiderate?—but this is what sharing a room is all about. You have to see it from both sides, be willing to compromise, and be considerate of the other person. Both of you have to do this.

3. BE READY. SHE'S GOING TO DO IT AGAIN.

After you have this conversation, I *guarantee* it will happen again. I'm telling you this so that you have realistic expectations. One conversation won't be enough. The key here is that *immediately* when it happens, you have to say something. You can't wait until morning or another day to rehash it. When she turns on the overhead light in the middle of the night, you need to, right then, speak up and say *kindly*, "Hey, Megan! Can you turn that off and...[whatever you agreed upon]?" If it happens multiple times, you'll need to bring it up like you did the first time. You have to commit to seeing the conflict through and finding resolution.

4. KNOW WHEN TO CALL IT QUITS.

The vast majority of the time, I see roommate conflicts completely destroy the relationship due to a simple lack of communication. Ninety percent of the time, people are reasonable, and they understand that they have to compromise and be considerate of others. *Occasionally*, this is not the case. Then and only then do I think it's okay to call it quits. Don't quit until you've genuinely tried to resolve the conflict and you've lived it out for at least the entire semester. You can do *anything* for three months. Frankly, I think you can do anything for nine months. Also keep in mind you could move into another room and have a whole different set of issues with that new roommate. You will be trading a known conflict for a set of unknown conflicts.

The bottom line is you're going to have conflict with any roommate. Always do your best to tackle the conflict head-on with open and honest communication. Anytime an issue arises, consider her perspective and then bring the matter up in an easy, nonattacking way. Always seek compromise, knowing you are never going to get 100 percent your way. Also, keep reminding yourself that when facing conflict and any relationship issues, you are using the opportunities God has given you to grow into the woman He has designed you to be—a reflection of Him in love, kindness, forgiveness, honesty, and more!

My Roommate's Boyfriend Is Over All the Time

Concern 16

> "My roommate's boyfriend is over a lot. *A lot*
> a lot. What's appropriate protocol? Do I hang
> out with them like I do when it's just her, or
> do I let them have their alone time? If they're
> just hanging out in the living room, is it okay
> if I join? I'm just not sure how I'm supposed
> to act with them as a couple as compared to
> just her."

This scenario rears its ugly head more times than you'd think. Of course we all want our dorm room or apartment to be a place where we can host friends or significant others, but when those spaces are typically small, it's easy to get overwhelmed when a roommate's guest appears frequently. Even worse is to feel like you need to be scarce because your roommate has guests or her boyfriend over. I know from experience how frustrating it can be when your roomie's boyfriend starts seeming more like a third roommate than a guest. This often strains a roommate situation and friendship, but it doesn't have to. Like with all roommate conflicts, the best solution boils down to honest and open communication with your roomie.

First things first. Is it okay for you to join your roomie and her BF while they're lounging in the common space? Absolutely! If you want to hang out around them or join in on whatever Netflix bingeing they're into, go for it! This is your living space too. If your roommate is dying for alone time with her boyfriend, it doesn't need to be in your common space.

Now, having said that, we have to remember that it is her home too. So if she wants to have a date night at home (maybe they cook dinner and want to watch a movie, just the two of them), she needs to discuss that with you ahead of time. It doesn't mean she can banish you from your apartment, but it does mean she can coordinate with you when you already have plans and don't anticipate being home around dinnertime. Just think about what you would want if the roles were reversed.

Regardless, you need to have a conversation with her about this. Don't panic—it doesn't have to be formal or serious. Plan a lunch with her and, at some point, bring up the topic. I would start by saying, "So I would love to hear your thoughts on something. I love hanging out with you, and I love hanging out with you and your boyfriend, but I'm curious what your expectations are. Is it okay that I hang out with you guys when he's over? How do you think it's been going?" Now, obviously you need to be honest here. So don't say you love hanging out with her or both of them if you don't. Or perhaps you're leaving them alone more than not, so, instead, you admit, "I feel like I'm tiptoeing around you guys a bit, because I'm not sure if it's okay for me to hang out. I don't want to cramp your style, but I also don't want to be hiding in my room. What do you think?" Ask open-ended questions and see how she responds.

During the conversation, it's important to talk through specifics. "So when I come home and find you guys hanging out in the living room, is it fair to assume I can join you if I want to?" Set up protocols, like "If I come home and you two are having a serious conversation, just say 'Mind giving us a minute?' and I'll know that means you need to be alone until I hear otherwise." The important thing is to think through times when you wondered if it was okay to join them and talk through those so you will know in the future what her expectations are.

Of course, all of this assumes your roommate has realistic expectations and is going to be respectful of you. For those of you who may have a situation where your roommate isn't considerate, this is where you really need to be open and honest about how her actions make you feel. Both of you need to consider what it would feel like to be in the other person's shoes. Sometimes, we get a roommate who simply doesn't care how her behavior affects you, and you are going to have to work hard to communicate honestly (but kindly), set firm boundaries, and be the bigger person. As I've already said, in those difficult roommate situations, you can only control you.

These are the moments when we get to practice giving grace and undeserved love to people. God uses life circumstances and relationships to refine us all through life. Learning to communicate openly and love others well (by being gracious and kind but also setting firm boundaries) will only behoove you in the long run. God will also use it to mold you to look much more like His Son.

My Roommate Is Having Sex All the Time

Concern 17

> "Every weekend I come home to my dorm to
> find I've been locked out because my room-
> mate has a guy over. I end up having to sleep
> on a friend's couch, instead of in my own bed.
> I'm exhausted and fed up."

Personally, and thankfully, I never had a roommate who put me in this situation. I did, however, have several friends who ended up crashing in my bedroom because their roommate wasn't as considerate. I'm not going to sugarcoat this: This is a crummy situation, where you don't have a ton of power.

If your roommate dearest is "locking" you out of your room, whether she is somehow literally locking you out or, more likely, blocking you out by sending a "don't come home" text, you are probably dealing with a roommate who just doesn't care how her actions impact you. It's not rocket science for her to think through her actions and realize what she is doing to you is just rude. She's the hardest roommate to have, because it means open communication and sound reasoning will rarely result in changed behavior.

That's the bad news.

The good news is that this is another opportunity for you to learn to control yourself, communicate in conflict, give grace when it's undeserved, and ask God to help you. I know that may sound insane, but it's the best option you have. It's similar to Concern

14 ("Dirty Dishes, Stolen Food, and Other Things That Drive You Crazy"). You can let this situation cause you to turn into the Wicked Witch of the West or someone who whines and complains every weekend about how lousy her roommate is, or you can refuse to let it steal your joy and choose to respond like Jesus would.

Seriously, imagine that for a second. What would it have looked like if Jesus had chosen to come to earth in the early twenty-first century? He didn't start His ministry until He was thirty years old. So He probably would have gone to college—and I bet He wouldn't have gone to a private religious school either. Considering how He loved to hang with the known sinners of His time, I imagine today Jesus would have attended the traditional state university, with football, tailgating, and all. In fact, He probably would have had a roommate who blocked Him from His own room from time to time!

How do you think Jesus would have responded? Do you remember the story in John 8, about Jesus and the adulterous woman? If you do, then you know that Jesus was teaching in the synagogue, and the Pharisees (the ruling religious leaders of the time) brought out a woman, probably a naked woman, and threw her in front of Jesus and the crowd, saying, "We caught her in the act of adultery! The law of Moses says to stone her. What say you?" One of my favorite things to do when reading the gospels is to watch how people interact with Jesus and then how He responds. Rarely does He respond the way we expect Him to. Instead of immediately replying to their question, He crouches down toward the ground and begins to write words in the dust with His fingers. No one knows what Jesus wrote, though lots of people have speculated. Since the Bible doesn't tell us, I figure we don't need to know. What happens next is more important. All of the Pharisees condemning this woman, who were ready and eager to stone her, walk away. Then Jesus turns to the woman and says,

"Where are your accusers? Didn't even one of them condemn you?" "No, Lord," she said. And Jesus said, "Neither do I. Go and sin no more." (John 8:10–11, NLT)

Now, let's get a few things straight. I am not saying your roommate is the adulterous woman. I also realize her actions are not preventing Jesus from going to sleep in His own bed. But think about this for a minute. Whom was the adulterous woman truly offending? Whom did her sin offend? God. Our sin is offensive to God, and yet Jesus, who was fully God and fully man, chose not to be offended or condemn her, but instead He responded with compassion, care, and concern. Jesus cared about her heart.

I know you and I aren't Jesus, but Jesus tells us over and over and over in the gospels to do what He did: *Follow my commands. Do what I say. Teach what I do.* So what would Jesus do if He had your roommate and your problem?

Well, I don't think Jesus was a doormat. He didn't let people walk all over Him, and He doesn't ask us to do that either. So, similar to the solution to Concern 15 ("She's Drunk and Loud, and I'm Just over Here Trying to Sleep!"), I think it's fair to say you should talk to your roommate. Be honest, compromise, come up with a plan, and be ready for her to do it again. Every true roommate conflict needs to be addressed with those first few steps. However, as I said at the very beginning, my bet is that your roommate just doesn't care how her actions impact you. That's unfortunate, but I truly meant it when I said that the good news is you have an opportunity to control yourself, communicate in conflict, give grace when it's undeserved, and ask God to help you.

Ask God to help you care more about your roommate's heart than about sleeping in your bed. I know that sounds radical, but I think that's the heart of God.

Do you need to take care of yourself? Absolutely. So you may need to find a weekend getaway, or maybe you need to find a new roommate and move out. Or maybe you decide to be brash and knock on the door loudly, give them a five-minute warning, and simply go into your room after five minutes. You can stick up for yourself and still be kind. But don't respond to rudeness with uglier rudeness. Ask God to help you respond like He would. You can't change your roommate, but I know someone who can. Ask Him. Pray about it and watch Him change your heart too!

I Gained a Roommate but Lost a Friend

Concern 18

"Last year my roommate (roomie #1) and I got along so well we decided to live together again this year. We also asked one of my friends (roomie #2) to live with us. Now, roomie #1 is always cooped up in her room while roomie #2 and I are getting along perfectly. We have people over. We cook together, shop together, and work out together. I just really don't know what to do about roomie #1. We used to be such good friends, and now I have to beg her to talk to me. When I ask her if something is wrong, she is super short."

Sadly, this happens a lot. Three girls can be tricky; whether it's three close friends or three roommates, someone often feels left out. One of two things is probably going on with your roomie. The first possibility is that she is feeling left out and her feelings are hurt. In my experience, this is often the case. You lived together last year, loved each other, and decided to live together again this year, but the addition of another friend complicated things. Regardless of your intentions or actual behavior, roomie #1 feels slighted. She thinks you like your other roommate better than her, and it hurts her feelings.

If this is not the case, then something bigger could be going on: depression, homesickness, anxiety, family issues . . . something else much greater than your friendship dynamics. When people hide in their rooms and retreat from their friends and family, it is a huge red flag that something deeply emotional or psychological is going on.

A good indicator of what's really going on is whether or not she is engaging with other people. Has she shut only you out or has she shut everyone out? If she has shut everyone out, it's definitely a bigger issue than just having her feelings hurt due to the addition of your second roommate. Otherwise, this is a classic case of the female trio problem.

So what's a girl to do?

YOU'RE GOING TO SHOW CARE AND CONCERN.

Next time she is home, cooped up in her room, knock on her door and ask if you can come in and talk for a few minutes. Get on her level. I mean this quite literally. If she is sitting on her bed, sit on a chair (or on her bed if she's okay with that) to be eye level with her. Or sit on the floor. What you don't want to do is stand up and look down on her while you're talking. This is a Confrontation 101 trick. Always be at eye level with or lower than the person you are confronting.

START BY ASSUMING THAT THIS IS JUST AN ISSUE OF HER FEELING LEFT OUT.

Begin your conversation by telling her you've noticed her withdrawing. Give specific examples. "It seems you're always in your room, not talking to me, not wanting to hang out, etc." This isn't to be accusatory; this is to show that you are paying attention and you *see her*. Tell her you feel like you've lost her as a friend, and ask if there was something you did that hurt her feelings. It may take a few promptings from you to get her to talk, but reiterate over and over that you didn't intend to hurt her and you'd really like to know if there was something you did so that you can fix it. Using phrases like "it feels like" or "it seems" is better than saying "you are." It comes off as less accusatory and more like your opinion. Again, you're not trying to smack down your roommate here! You want her to feel like you are on her team.

IF SHE SAYS, "NO, EVERYTHING'S FINE," YOU CAN'T FORCE HER TO TALK.

Reiterate that you miss her and want your friend back! Tell her that you are concerned about her, and if she decides that there is something she wants to address with you, ask her to let you know. Tell her that you are going to go out of your way to make sure she knows she is invited (to cook, hang out, work out, etc.) anytime you are doing something with your other roomie. And then you actually have to do that. So don't tell her that if you don't plan on following through.

ASK IF ANYTHING ELSE IS GOING ON.

There may be a larger issue at hand. If there is, give her an opportunity to tell you about it. "Is there anything else going on? It just seems like something's different this year.... Is everything okay?" Again, you can't force her to talk, so the goal is for you to express your care and concern and your willingness to listen and talk whenever she desires.

IF IT'S LOOKING MORE AND MORE LIKE THERE IS SOMETHING BIGGER GOING ON, CONSIDER PULLING IN SOMEONE ELSE SHE TRUSTS AND WILL LISTEN TO.

Sometimes we have to surround people from all sides to get them to admit they need help. Maybe you just need to pull in another good friend of hers to have a similar conversation. Sometimes when we are in a dark place, we need multiple friends to reach out before we are able to admit we need help.

Find out if your school offers free counseling or how to see a counselor, and have that option in your back pocket if she is ready. Maybe she doesn't want to share with you what is going on, but she admits she does need to talk to someone. Offer to walk with her to the counseling center for her first appointment. Sit in the waiting room with her if that would make her feel comfortable. If she really is struggling with something major and you communicate your care and concern, she will eventually feel safe enough to let you in. Then you just have to be the supportive friend I know you are!

However, until she is ready to communicate with you, there is nothing more you can do. So do your part by sitting down with her and trying to talk it out, but then it's up to her. No matter what's going on, she has to come to a place where she is willing to be open and honest. Show her you care and want to fix your relationship and see where that takes you. If she doesn't open up, that's okay. It's not your burden to bear. Pray for her and remind yourself that God cares about her way more than you do, and He will carry her through this.

When Is It Okay to Consider Switching Roommates?

Concern 19

> "My roommate and I just aren't compatible. I have to move out of this room and get away from her!"

It's your first semester of freshman year, you're a month into college, and you are daydreaming about poisoning your roommate. Oh, that was just me? Well, you're a better human than I was, but you may still be wondering if there's some way you can switch rooms as soon as possible. Let me caution you. Unless things are just awful in your room, I highly encourage you to try to make it a full year with your roommate.

Why on earth would you do that? Well, for a few reasons:

1. IT WILL GROW YOU AND MATURE YOU IMMENSELY.

I know I've already said this several times, but learning to live with roommates is one of the most refining processes we go through in college. Sure, it'd be easier to just bail when things are less than ideal, but if you can stick it out and learn to live with someone who isn't your best friend, someone who even gets on your nerves, you will learn so much about patience, kindness, graciousness, communication, and more. I realize it doesn't seem the most practical choice to stick it out with a difficult roommate just so you can learn something. Who does that?! But have you considered that God is completely in control of your life and may have actually given you the roommate you have for a reason? He's over everything, is He not? So is He over the roommate assignment process? I think so. I'm not trying to overspiritualize your roommate assignment, but I do think it's worth considering: *Does God have a greater purpose for me in this roommate situation, and am I missing out by running away from it?*

2. IT'S PRACTICAL.

It's usually tough to switch midyear. So unless you have a close friend whose roommate happens to be moving out and leaving an easy spot for you to fill, I'd highly consider staying put. You are welcome to talk to your RA or hall director and see what kind of options you may have, but for the many years I worked in Residence Life there was rarely a vacancy for someone to move into due to roommate problems. Instead of daydreaming about your escape plan, maybe it's worth finding out if there is actually a better destination. If not, it will be easier for you to settle back in and continue working on your current roommate relationship.

3. WHEN YOU SWITCH ROOMMATES, YOU ARE TRADING A SET OF KNOWN PROBLEMS FOR A SET OF UNKNOWN PROBLEMS.

You already know the things that grate on you and the problems you have to work through with your current roomie. However, you don't know what this new roommate situation will be like—even if she is your sorority sister. Remember, best friends can sometimes be horrible roommates. Every roommate situation comes with a set of challenges, no matter how perfect it seems at first. Switching roommates could open a whole new bag of problems that are even worse than what you're facing now.

At least give it a full semester, because if I could last an entire nine months with Shannon, you can stay with your roommate too!

How Do I Tell My Roommate I Don't Want to Live with Her Again?
Concern 20

"My roommate wants to live with me again next year, but I don't know how to tell her no. I don't want to hurt her feelings!"

Your roommate is sweet and nice, but she drives you crazy. Maybe she's always in the room, or she's super messy or loud, or is always eating your food, or your schedules are polar opposites. Maybe she's fine but you want to live with another friend. Whatever your reasoning may be, you have decided you'd rather not live with her again next year.

First, let me say, that is totally okay! While I often push back on girls when they want to change roommates midyear, it is absolutely fine for you to break the news to your current roomie that you have other plans next year. But before we get into the steps of how to do that, I want to speak to the girl who is wondering if it's worth potentially hurting your roommate's feelings so you can live with someone else.

I know you don't want to hurt her feelings or harm a friendship, but if you really would rather not live with her again, you need to follow your gut. If you don't and you choose to suck it up and live with her another year, let me tell you why that's not the best plan.

YOU WILL RESENT HER.
By October of next year, you are going to completely resent her. The things that slightly annoy you today will grow from small hills

into giant mountains. The waves of tiny tension you currently experience will become vast valleys of conflict within another year.

ANY CHANCE OF HAVING A FRIENDSHIP WITH HER WILL BE GONE.

I know you don't want to hurt her feelings, and you certainly don't want to damage a friendship. While the initial conversation may be awkward, and you may still hurt her feelings at first, if you part ways now, you could actually maintain your friendship. I've seen numerous situations like these turn out for the best. But if you choose to stay roommates, you will resent her, and resentment leads to a broken friendship.

YOU WILL NEVER WANT TO GO BACK TO YOUR ROOM.

Don't put yourself in that situation. It's not freshman-year random-roommate assignment anymore. Hopefully, you can make decisions that will give you a great living environment where you like to hang out and study. Don't agree to live with this girl again and then spend the next nine months avoiding her and your room.

YOU ARE DOING YOURSELF A DISSERVICE BY NOT PRACTICING CONFRONTATION.

Yes, confrontation is hard, but you will have to do it your whole life. Start practicing now. Remember, this is an opportunity for you to grow. It's also an opportunity for her to grow! You have no idea how God may use this in her life—whether it's learning how to respond to a hard conversation or, more likely, giving her an experience with a new roommate who will grow her in different ways.

YOU ARE NOT BEING NICE TO HER.

I know that you don't want to hurt her, so you think the nice thing to do is to suck it up and live with her again. However, you're not being kind by essentially lying to her and pretending that you still want to room together. What if you tell her the truth—that she needs to make plans to live with someone else—and that ends up being even better for her? Don't you think she could find a better roommate for herself? One who actually wants to live with her? I bet she can.

You know I'm right, but it doesn't take that sick feeling away when you think about telling her. So this is what you're going to do:

1. **Set a deadline for yourself.** Tell yourself, *By this Friday at noon, I'm going to tell Rachel that I don't want to room with her again.* Tell a trusted friend or family member your plan and ask them to keep you accountable. Also, keep in mind, the sooner, the better. She needs to start making new plans for her living situation.

2. **Schedule a time with her to talk.** Ask her out to coffee or lunch, or even set up a time to talk in the room. You just want to make sure it's a good time for her and you're sending a signal that you need to discuss something important. Just say, "Hey, Rachel, do you have some free time tonight? I want to talk to you about something." When she says, "Uh, yeah, I'll be done with class by eight," you say, "Great! I'll meet you here. Maybe we can go grab a coffee." You can keep it casual, but by setting up a time, you're giving her a heads-up. If she asks, "What's this about?" say, "I've just been thinking about next year and want to talk about it with you." That may give her an idea of where the conversation is headed, which isn't a bad thing. The last thing you want to do is totally take her by surprise or wait so last-minute that you really put her in a bind.

3. **Have the talk.** What are you going to say? Think through what you want to communicate to her about why you don't want to live together. In my opinion, a great reason is, "I want to stay

friends with you and I think we'd be better friends if we weren't also roommates." Sometimes great friends are horrible roommates. Of course, if you don't want to be friends with her next year, don't use that one. I've also heard things like, "As I'm thinking about my living situation next year, I feel like I need to do something different—I want to find someone [who has a similar schedule to mine, who is as big of a neat freak as I am, who is . . . whatever]." Or maybe it's as simple as saying, "Ashley and I have been talking, and we decided we want to live together." Just pick *one* reason and stick to it. You don't need to have a laundry list of five hundred things that drive you crazy about her. Make sure you reiterate that you care about her and don't want to hurt her feelings. Say that this has been a really hard decision but you feel like this is what's best for you. Apologize if you do hurt her feelings, and tell her that is not your intention—because it's not your intention, right? You don't want to hurt her feelings.

But, news flash, you don't make her feel. It took me years to learn this. I control my actions and I am responsible for my feelings. You control your actions and are responsible for your feelings. So you are not responsible for how she feels. You can care about her feelings, but you can't take them on as your responsibility. As long as you communicate openly with kindness, you are not at fault. So set a deadline for yourself, tell someone you trust to keep you accountable, and then tell your roommate that you love and care about her but think it's best if you don't live together again. Practice confrontation and honest communication. You are doing yourself and your roommate a favor. I promise.

"Okay. But what if I have two roommates right now and only want to live with one of them next year?"

Or you want to ditch your roommate but live with your other suitemates. Or some kind of combo where you are including some but leaving others out.

Well, all is fair in love and war—or roommate situations—but, like the steps we just covered, let's do it in a way where we care for your roomie as best we can.

First, you don't know what you're working with until you have heard from all relevant parties. Don't start the conversation with your agenda. Simply ask each girl what she is planning to do next year.

Second, if you and your one roommate are in agreement that you want to live without the third, you must communicate this to her in the kindest way possible. Don't gang up on her. Don't make her feel inferior. However, you also can't lead her on or not bring up the situation until it's too late in the game. Be up-front. If you avoid telling her or make secret plans behind her back, you are lying to her and hurting her. Think about how you would want to be treated if the roles were reversed.

Finally, if your other roommate does want to live with your third roommate and they want you to join them, you have a decision to make. You will need to carefully weigh your options and decide if living with the "good" roomie is worth living with the other. If you do decide to live with them both, you will have to check your attitude. Don't set yourself up to be bitter or resentful toward the "other" roommate. She hasn't done anything to intentionally hurt or annoy you. You are going to have to learn to let go, not let little things get under your skin, and treat her with kindness and respect. Of course, your other option is to not live with either of them and find a new roommate. What is not an option, in my opinion, is convincing the "good" roomie to live with you and ditch the other. That is manipulative and selfish. Again, how would you feel if the roles were reversed?

One of my very favorite verses in the Bible, and also one of the most convicting for me, was written by Paul: "Do nothing from selfish ambition or conceit, but in humility count others more significant than yourselves. Let each of you look not only to his own interests, but also to the interests of others" (Phil. 2:3–4 ESV). Anytime I find myself in a conflict or point of tension with another person, this verse comes to mind. What does it look like for me to count another person as more important than myself? What does it look like for me to think of their interests and not just my own? The verse doesn't say: Deny your own interests and only act in such a way that benefits another person's interests. It simply says: Don't just think about yourself; think about others.

What does it look like for you to think about your roommate's interests? It doesn't mean you have to live with her again, but it does mean you need to imagine how you would want to be treated if you were in her shoes. You need to be as full of kindness, grace, and love as you can be in regard to when and how you talk to her about this.

My Roommate Has Her Own Group of Friends, and I Feel Left Out

Concern 21

> "My roommate has her own solid group of friends to hang out with, and I still don't know anyone. I've tried to tag along a few times, but it feels like she'd rather not include me. I don't want to seem needy, but I'm just not sure what to do."

Let me start by saying I'm sorry. It stinks to feel left out. It hurts to feel lonely. And it's doubly hard when your roommate has her own friend group established and you don't.

I know you may also be hurt that your roommate isn't inviting you when she goes out with her friends. My guess is that she's not being malicious. She's not leaving you out to intentionally hurt you. Remind yourself of that. We have to believe the best of people. While she may be aware that it's weird or awkward when she doesn't invite you, I can't imagine that she really wants to hurt you.

All that said, you've got to find your own friends. While it'd be nice if your roommate included you, don't you want to create your own community? I know that's a lot more work than glomming on to her friend group, but you need to find your own people. So let's get to it.

How are you going to find your friends? This week you are going to:

1. **Chum it up with people who sit near you in your classes.** I know this may seem awkward, but you just have to

do it. Talk to them and get to know them. You may be sitting next to your future best friend! Or if you don't love the people you sit next to but you've noticed a girl on the other side of the room who has a friendly face, go sit next to her. Look around the spaces you're in and observe people. Look for people you want as your friends.

2. **If you have time immediately following a class, ask classmates you've hit it off with if they want to join you for lunch or a coffee break.** Be an initiator. Most people are just looking for a leader to follow. Everyone wants friends, but few act as the initiator. Be the initiator.

3. **Say yes anytime you are asked to hang out socially.** Okay, you need to do your homework, but seriously, don't turn down most invites. You have to say yes a lot at first to find your people. If you're constantly saying, "No, thanks," when invited out, you are limiting yourself in regard to experiences and people. You are also creating a reputation as a "no girl." People stop asking no girls if they want to hang. When you do need to say no, make sure you're expressing that you wish you could and give a good reason, like you have to finish your history paper. If people think you're turning them down so you can stay in and binge-watch Netflix, they are going to write you off.

4. **Find a handful of student organizations that interest you and start attending their meetings and events.** Do this faithfully. Show up consistently. When you're there, take the initiative to meet people and make connections. Student organizations are a great place to find your people because you know you have at least one similar interest. My very best friends all came from the student organizations I was involved in: Residence Life, an a cappella group, a Christian ministry, and even a sociology club.

5. **Initiate time to hang out with other people on your hall.**
   Do this at least every two or three days, but really as much
   as possible. It doesn't have to be planned out. It could mean
   that at 6:15 p.m., when you're hungry for dinner, you just walk
   down your hall and find people who want to go grab dinner
   with you. Everyone needs to eat, and a lot of other people are
   sitting in their rooms, wishing they had dinner plans too. Be
   the one who finds those people and include them.

Are you seeing the theme here? **You have to initiate.** You have
to pursue others. Ask people to grab coffee, go for a walk, grab a
meal, go to the gym with you, etc. Set a goal for yourself—*I will
ask ____ people to hang out this week*—and do it. Make plans to
do things that you like to do, and find someone to do them with
you. Right now, come up with three people whom you can ask to
do something with you in the next three days. If they say no, ask
again another time.

One final note, going back to the circumstance at hand with
your roommate: Be kind to her. Don't make her feel bad for not including you. Be the bigger person. Then, when you've made plans
with other people (because you're going to be an initiator), invite
her occasionally. She probably feels guilty for not inviting you all
the time, but she is probably also fighting the feeling of being ob-
ligated to invite you. She doesn't want to feel socially responsible
for you. Which, of course, she doesn't need to be, because you are
completely able to take care of yourself. My guess is that once she
sees you creating your own community, she may actually start including you more. Sounds crazy, but I see it happen all the time.
She needs to feel like you are independent from her. More than
likely she fears that you depend on her, and that is causing her to
not include you in her own plans.

But this isn't about her. It's about you. Go start making friends this week and be patient with the process. It will take time for you to find really great friends, but you have to initiate and pursue a ton of people. Best friends don't fall out of the sky. You make them. You cultivate those relationships.

Finally, pray about it. Seriously. God will honor your prayers. Ask Him for some great friends. I think you'll find He delights in giving you things like that.

My Roommate Just Told Me She's Gay

Concern 22

It was only a few months into the school year, and Macey, my roommate, decided it was time to tell me she was bisexual. She had been in a serious relationship with a girlfriend for about a year, but it had ended a couple of months after we became roommates. She believed love was love—regardless of gender—and wanted me to know.

To this day, I'm not actually sure why she told me. Was she trying to get a reaction out of me? See what I thought about homosexuality? Was she truly just trying to be transparent? I don't know. I also have no recollection of what I said to her that day. My guess is something to the effect of "Cool. Thanks for telling me."

I do remember, after that conversation, thinking through what her sexual orientation meant for our living environment. I was semi-modest, but I changed clothes pretty openly in our bedroom. Was I still comfortable doing that? Was she checking me out?

I decided pretty quickly that Macey's bisexual declaration didn't change anything. I felt confident she wasn't checking me out when I undressed, and if "love is love" for Macey, well, I could have guaranteed she never would have fallen in love with me. So despite the fact that she may have been attracted to women, I didn't feel threatened or uncomfortable.

Typically, when college girls approach me with a similar scenario—their roommate comes out to them as bisexual or gay—they are trying to work through one or all of these questions:

- Am I comfortable living with someone who is attracted to women?
- If I believe homosexuality is a sin, can I live with someone who identifies as gay?
- Should I move out? Is it okay for me to move out?
- How do I love my roommate well, whether or not I agree with her lifestyle, but also factor in my own well-being?

All of these are fair questions to be asking.

I'm not going to take this moment to try to convince you that homosexuality is or is not a sin. While I do think it's important for you to grapple with what the Bible says about homosexuality, it honestly doesn't matter in this particular moment, because the question is not *What does God think about my roommate's beliefs or lifestyle?* It's *How do I share a room with someone who is attracted to my gender?*

Now, if you do believe the Bible condemns homosexuality and you're trying to wrap your brain around this, let me explain why now is not the time to confront your roommate about it.

For one, if your roommate isn't a believer in Jesus, it's never the time. Jesus didn't call sinners to Him by starting with, "Stop sinning and then follow Me!" He called people to Himself with "I love you. I want to be in a relationship with you. Follow Me. Obey Me. Sin no more." Jesus lovingly extends the same offer to each of us. No matter our sin, He meets us where we are. In the same way, we shouldn't try to convince our non-Christian friends not to have sex before marriage. We shouldn't confront nonbelievers about the sin in their life. The Holy Spirit does that.

This is another reason why you shouldn't tell a sinner who doesn't know Jesus to stop sinning: Christianity isn't about behavior modification. It's about a heart modification. The Bible says God makes us into new creations. It's as if He completely changes our DNA so that we can obey Him and follow His commands. But we can't ask someone who hasn't had a change of heart to change their behavior.

Furthermore, if your roommate is a believer and identifies as gay, you may want to have a conversation about it another time, but you have to earn that right. Even if my roommate Macey had been a believer, I was not in the position to have that discussion with her when she made her declaration. We had only known each other for a few months and we weren't friends; we were tolerable roommates. A tolerable roommate has not earned the right to speak hard truths and ask hard questions of someone else.

Occasionally, you will find yourself in a relationship with another believer who is not living according to God's will, and you may have to say something out of care and concern for that person. But those conversations can happen only between two people who love each other, trust each other, and have built a strong foundation of friendship. Otherwise, the conversation goes nowhere. I am not going to be called out of some sin or bad decision I'm making by someone who barely knows me. I have been called out of sin by friends who love me deeply and have walked many years beside me. They earned the right to speak into my life, and I trusted them enough to consider what they had to say.

But back to the original question at hand: *How do I share a room with someone who is attracted to my gender?*

Maybe your situation is more like mine was. You realize your roommate is not girl-obsessed. She's not checking you out while you undress. She's not attracted to you or crushing on you. You don't feel threatened or uncomfortable and you conclude it's not that big a deal.

But maybe it is a big deal. While I often advocate for girls to hang in there and stick it out with their imperfect roommate, the most important thing for both of you is that you have a safe place to rest your head. If your roommate situation is causing you anxiety to the point that you avoid your room at all costs, have trouble sleeping, or find it negatively impacting your studies and social life, it's time to make a decision that is best for you. Talk to your RA or hall director and see what other options may be available.

No matter what you decide, it's still just as important that you treat your roommate with kindness, love, and respect, just like in any other roommate conflict. She is a creation of God. He loves her. In fact, He's crazy about her and He really cares about her heart. So as you decide what to do and what's going to be best for you, ask God to give you His eyes. Ask Him to help you see her the way He sees her. Ask Him to help you talk to her and treat her the way He would. Whether she is a believer or not, the way you respond to her coming out will speak volumes about who you are and who your God is. That doesn't mean you have to continue being her roommate, but it does mean you need to be careful and remember we are ambassadors of Jesus in all situations, including this one.

CHAPTER SIX

Friends, Best Friends + Boyfriends

College Girl Concerns 23–31

I would rather walk with a friend in the dark
than walk alone in the light.

—Helen Keller

You and I were designed by God for connection. He created us to learn intimacy in a variety of forms, through family, friends, and significant others. While it's exciting to start a new chapter of life where you are able to redefine who you are and who your community will be, it's actually much harder than you may anticipate to create meaningful relationships in college. It's surprising to be surrounded by people every minute of the day and yet still feel alone and unknown. Part of college is learning how to pursue and create great friendships. Another part is learning how to manage difficult relationships with people who may drive you crazy or even hurt you.

Of course, we'd be remiss if we didn't talk about the one relationship many college girls are hoping for: one with their future husband. You *could* meet your husband in college, but I have to break it to you that you very well may not. Regardless, college is a time for you to learn how to be wise in friendships, how to date, and how to wait for Mr. Right instead of latching on to Mr. Right Now.

Where Are All My College Besties?

Concern 23

> "I came to college under the impression that I would meet my lifelong best friends here. So far, the friends I have made are fine, but where's my best friend? I still feel a little lost."

It took me a while to find my people my freshman year of college. Initially, my friends were people I had met in my orientation group and girls who lived on my hall. I was also around a group of girls who attended a weekly Bible study, but I didn't press into those relationships very much. It wasn't until the end of the school year that I started to feel like I had found some real full-heart friendships. But then I transferred and had to start all over again! Looking back on freshman year, I am certain there were folks who could have become lifelong friends. However, meaningful friendships take time, and I had only been pursuing those relationships for a few months.

You have to remind yourself of the same thing. Finding your best friend takes time, patience, and a lot of effort. Like me, you may not cross paths with your besties until a year or two into college. At the risk of sounding like a broken record, let me remind you...

YOU ARE NOT ALONE.

There are so many other people who feel like you do, who wonder how to make friends, and who feel lonely. We all go through seasons like this. This is normal. This is part of college, and this is part of the rest of your life. You will forever find yourself in new situations, where you have to start the friend-making process all over again.

NO MATTER WHAT STAGE OF LIFE YOU'RE IN, YOU HAVE TO CONTINUE PURSUING NEW FRIENDSHIPS.

You do this when you start college; you do it again when you start your first professional job. You'll do it again when you move and again when your best friend moves. You'll do it again when you get married and look for couple friends. You'll do it again if you go to graduate school. We are never in a season of life where we stop making friends. Since college, I have found myself in the friend-making phase seven times due to situations like the ones I just listed. Seven times! Most recently was when I had been living in Nashville for more than five years and realized most of my best friends had all moved away. Suddenly, my core group was down to just me, and I needed to find a new set of Nashville girlfriends.

THE FIRST STEP TO FINDING YOUR BEST FRIENDS IS KNOWING WHO YOU ARE.

What are your values and beliefs? What are your interests? How do you like to spend your time? You need to know these things about yourself. Of course, we are constantly evolving, so I'm not saying you have to have everything figured out. But you do have to feel comfortable in your own skin. It's really hard to make friends with others when you aren't comfortable with yourself or, like in the great Julia Roberts chick flick *Runaway Bride*, when you don't know how you like your eggs.

I believe this was a piece of my problem my freshman year. It wasn't that I didn't know who I was, but I just really wanted to fit in. So my plan was to hang with whoever wanted to be friends with me and camouflage my true self to get along. Friendships based on convenience are usually not deep, lifelong, full-heart friendships. Once I decided I wanted to be fully me, I started looking for (and finding!) friends who would encourage that.

LOOK FOR LIKE-MINDED PEOPLE.

Once you've figured out how you like your eggs or, to skip the analogy, who you are and what you like/dislike, then you look for like-minded people. I'm not saying you can't have friends who are the polar opposite of you, but you start with people who share some similarities. You have to find people you're comfortable around and who encourage you to continue being you.

Chin up, my friend. Take this opportunity to get to know yourself and decide what kind of friend you want to be. Then pursue others who allow you to be fully you. Keep reading. The next section—Concern 24—is applicable to everyone!

I'm a Transfer Student: How Do I Join Already-Formed Friend Groups?
Concern 24

"My college is known for being cliquey. How do I join friend groups that have already been formed?"

This is a great question that is applicable whether you're a freshman, a transfer student, or simply looking for new friends! Most of the time when we are the new kid on the block, whether we're in a new church, a new town, or a new job environment, we have to finagle our way into an already-existing community or friend group. Of course, this can be easier or harder depending on the openness of the people we are trying to befriend, but so much is up to you and your determination to pursue people.

When I transferred my sophomore year, I realized pretty quickly that either I could get lumped into the freshman crowd or I could chase after other sophomores and upperclassmen and try to convince them to be my friends. Typically, it's pretty easy to find friends your freshman year. They may be friends of convenience and not lifelong friends, but everyone shows up to college as a freshman needing to find friends. So you're all in the same boat, and it's rarely difficult to find someone who wants to hang out. But when you transfer and you don't want to hang with the freshies (no offense, freshmen), you really have to pursue your peers. Upperclassmen typically have already formed their friend groups. A much smaller number are still in pursuit of new friends. And that just means you have to work a little harder.

*   *   *

The most important thing is that you commit to being persistent and choosing to believe the best of others. Here are my four rules of thumb when it comes to pursuing new friends.

1. ASK PEOPLE OUT FOR COFFEE OR LUNCH, TO RUN ERRANDS WITH YOU, OR TO GO TO A WORKOUT CLASS OR WHATEVER ACTIVITY YOU ENJOY.

I've never been a large-group person. I tend to get overwhelmed with groups larger than six. I love getting to know people and connecting on a deeper level, and I just find that rather impossible to do when hanging out in a large group. So as you think about pursuing new relationships and friend groups, remember that it's much easier to get to know one person individually rather than to join a group outing with a bunch of friends who already know one another well. If you get to know one or two people from an existing friend group on an individual level, they will eventually invite you to join in on group activities. But start at the individual level and see where it goes.

When I transferred, I knew a handful of people at my new school, one of whom was a close friend from high school. He did me the favor of "setting me up" with a handful of other girls he knew I would hit it off with. He introduced us, and then I took it upon myself to schedule a coffee or lunch with them to get to know them better. Two or three of the girls he connected me with ended up being some of my very best friends and even my roommates later on. Now, I know not everyone has the benefit of a good friend to set them up on friend dates, but it was still up to me to pursue those girls and develop true friendships. Eventually, they started asking me to hang out with their own friend groups, which widened my social circle, where I got to meet more like-minded people who became great friends.

2. YOU MAY HAVE TO ASK SOMEONE TO HANG OUT WITH YOU TEN TIMES BEFORE THEY EVER THINK TO RECIPROCATE AN INVITATION.

That's okay. When you already have a group of best friends, it's hard to remember to invite the new girl. People aren't being malicious; they just aren't thinking outside their normal friend group. So we have to have thick skin, not get offended if we aren't invited to something, and choose to believe the best of people.

3. BE A CONNECTOR.

Don't hoard all of your new friends to yourself. If you've gotten lunch a few times with a girl you think would also connect with another friend you've gotten to know, invite them both to do something with you. Sometimes people don't do this because they are afraid they will be cut out if the other two friends connect better. Again, choose to believe the best of people and be confident with what you have to offer. People prefer to be friends with connectors over people who isolate themselves with their close friends.

4. IT'S ALL ABOUT THE APPROACH.

Approach people (especially those who already have their friend group established) with an unspoken attitude of *I am a great friend to have and you want me as your friend. I am going to convince you of that.* It sounds silly, but that is the perspective you have to take. That was my aha moment as a transfer student. I had to prove to people that they wanted me as their friend. And eventually, I did. I made some of my closest friends as a transfer student—all of whom already had best friends and social groups formed. But it takes time, persistence, and a confidence that you have something great to offer to others. And you do have something great to offer. I know you do!

My Best Friends Are All Partying and Going Insane
Concern 25

> "My best friends from high school are all partying and going insane in college. How am I supposed to respond to them?"

All of us experience this one way or the other in college. Either we are the ones who go crazy or we are the ones who look at our friends and think, *What happened to you? How did you turn into this crazy person?* I've been both.

When my friends turned into binge-drinking party animals, I judged them. I was appalled by their behavior. They knew better—they were raised better than that—and I totally sat up on my pedestal and judged them.

It makes me sad today when I recall how I responded to them. Their sin may have been loud and evident, but mine was equally ugly. It was just hidden in the dark shadows of my heart, instead of out there for the world to see. While I may have "looked" better on the outside, I was in no place to judge them.

Then I decided to fix them. I'm a fixer. I love to solve problems, especially other people's problems and—let's just go ahead and say it—people. I love to think I can fix people. (Please note: THIS IS CRAZY TALK. The only person in the business of fixing people is JESUS. Not me or you.) So my Jesus-loving-turned-heathen friends (I mean, that's what I thought) became my project. I was totally consumed with trying to "save" them from their excessive partying and hookups. Please. It makes me cringe (and laugh) to think what a savior complex I really had. And, let me say, I was motivated by good intentions. I felt a burden for my friends. I was saddened by the choices they were making and I wanted to help them stop, in order to prevent further consequences. Because no matter what, my friends, there are always consequences when we get sucked into the binge-drinking culture, or anytime we decide our way seems more fun than Jesus' way.

Here's what I wish someone had told me while I was trying to save my friends:

IT'S NOT YOUR MONKEY.

Years ago, my mom told me this proverb about a monkey. The basic concept is that the big problem your friend is dealing with, well, that's her monkey. It's clinging to her back and climbing all over her and is really a bother. But the next thing you know, whether because she asked you to hold him for a second or because you offered to take him on (savior alert!), now YOU'VE got the monkey on your back. Suddenly the monkey is your problem. He's climbing all over you, demanding your attention, picking at your hair, smashing bananas on your arm, and the only way for you to get him off you is to pass him off to someone else (preferably the monkey's owner).

There was a season of my life when this idea became one of my top mantras: "Nope—not my monkey," I'd remind myself when considering how to save someone else. But oh, how I wish I'd known that concept back in college. Yes, your friends may be making stupid decisions, but at the end of the day, it's not your monkey. You cannot control anyone else's behavior or actions but your own. So stop trying. It's not your monkey.

THERE IS A RIGHT WAY TO CONFRONT.

Jesus actually gave us explicit details on how we should confront our Christian brothers and sisters:

If your brother or sister sins, go and point out their fault, just between the two of you. If they listen to you, you have won them over. But if they will not listen, take one or two others along, so that "every matter may be established by the testimony of two or three witnesses." If they still refuse to listen, tell it to the church; and if they refuse to listen even to the church, treat them as you would a pagan or a tax collector. (Matthew 18:15–17 NIV)

I love this passage because it's so clear, yet ironically, it's also a little tricky. First of all, Jesus says to talk to them directly. Don't go to all your other friends first and talk to them about how you need to talk to your other friend. Don't gossip. Don't ask for "prayer to talk with her"—a.k.a. the Christian way of gossiping. Just go talk to her! Then, if she doesn't listen, pull in another friend (a good, safe friend) who will also express concern. You could even go the next step of pulling in "the church" by asking a mentor or an old small-group leader to step in.

But my favorite part of this passage is the last line: "If they still refuse to listen...treat them as you would a pagan or a tax collector." This is where I think things get a little tricky. We think, *Ooooh. That means we kick them out of the church.* But how did Jesus treat tax collectors and pagans? He loved them! He ate meals with them. He went over to their homes. Jesus loved on and hung out with the pagans and tax collectors because that is the only way to shine God's light on others. We don't cast out the partiers or anyone else making bad decisions that go against what God wants for them. We love them and spend time with them.

James said it like this:

My brothers and sisters, if one of you should wander from the truth and someone should bring that person back, remember this: Whoever turns a sinner from the error of their way will save them from death and cover over a multitude of sins. (James 5:19–20 NIV)

Looking back, I sure wish someone had called me out when I was the one "going crazy." Did I survive it? Yes. Did I come back to living in obedience to Jesus? Yes. Do I have scars and consequences to prove it? I sure do. Maybe I'd have a few less scars if someone spoke up like Jesus told us to.

If your friends are going crazy in the party scene, do them a favor by loving them enough to speak truth into their lives (call them out!), but at the end of the day, it's not your monkey and Jesus loves them anyway. Don't let their behavior steal your joy. Be a truth teller, love them like crazy, and keep on with your own life, knowing you are responsible only for yourself.

Where's My Future Husband?
Concern 26

"I kind of thought I would meet my husband in
college, but so far I haven't dated anyone, and
it doesn't look like that's going to change anytime soon. I just thought I'd meet him here—
that's how my parents met!"

Whether we are up-front about it or even realize it, a lot of girls
have this expectation. My parents met in college, so while I wasn't
on the hunt to find my future husband, I definitely thought that's
how things would pan out. I mean, where else was I going to meet
him? I had a few love interests in college, but by my junior year
I was in a serious relationship with a guy and definitely thought I
was going to marry him. When we broke up, I was super confused.
Okay, I thought, *if it isn't him, maybe it's another guy friend
of mine.* Eventually, I graduated from college as a single girl, and
while I wasn't necessarily upset that I hadn't locked in a husband,
I was definitely still confused. While I didn't have ring-by-spring
fever, I still had to let go of the expectation that I'd be like my parents, who married soon after graduation.

Whether you're an incoming freshman or a graduating senior,
I strongly encourage you to just stop. Stop looking for your
future husband; stop wondering where he is. College should
not be about finding your spouse. That can certainly be a by-
product, but if you spend more time and energy thinking about
where your husband is than about your classes, your career

ambitions, your friendships, your campus involvement, your relationship with Jesus, and enjoying the season you're in, you are majorly missing out.

FIRST OF ALL, MEETING YOUR SPOUSE IN COLLEGE ISN'T THE NORM.

A study published in 2013 shows that the median age for women to get married is twenty-seven, and for men it's twenty-nine.[1] To think that you will meet your husband at the age of twenty and then not marry until your late twenties is insane. Much more likely, you'll meet him in your midtwenties through mutual friends. Facebook also published a report in 2013 that said 28 percent of married college grads (on Facebook) went to the same college as their spouse.[2] Of course, that doesn't necessarily mean they met their spouse in college. I have friends who married men from their (very large) alma mater, and though they went to college at the same time, they didn't meet each other until their mid to late twenties! But based on Facebook's data, you're looking at a one in four chance that you go to the same college as your spouse. Those aren't bad odds, but that's certainly not the majority. The majority is that three out of four people don't go to the same college as their future spouse.

My husband and I did not go to the same college, but if we had, I never would have given him the time of day! We didn't meet until we were twenty-seven; we didn't start dating until we were twenty-nine, and then we got married shortly after. While I'm sure I could have married some guy friend from college, I'm so glad I didn't. God knew just what He was doing when He introduced us in our late twenties. My husband is a tangible reminder in my life of how God's plan, His timing, and His provision are so much better than what I can create myself.

SECOND, YOU'RE SABOTAGING EVERY MALE RELATIONSHIP YOU HAVE.

If you look at every male friend as a potential boyfriend or future husband, you're hurting yourself and them! I had some of the best guy friends in college. I lived in a house with five other girls, and we had great guy friends who loved on us by mowing our lawn, changing our flat tires, shoveling our driveway after a snow, deicing our stairs—you name it, they did it! They took such great care of us. And you know what? Not one of us married any of the guys who did that. In fact, out of all six of us, only one went to college with her future husband, but they didn't begin dating until they were in their midtwenties.

If every time you meet a new guy you start imagining what your children will look like, you are allowing your head and heart to run down a very unhealthy road. Don't be the girl who thinks every first date is going to turn into marriage. Instead, focus on building healthy, meaningful friendships with guys. Be a good friend, not a husband scout!

THIRD AND FINALLY, YOU'RE JUST MISSING OUT.

As I said earlier, college is about so many wonderful things. Don't cheapen your experience by wasting time and energy on something that may not happen. Spend time cultivating your interests, developing career ambitions, building meaningful friendships, learning more about who God has designed you to be, learning more about God, serving others, having fun, and enjoying the season you're in!

This Guy Is Pursuing Me, and I'm Not Sure I'm into Him

Concern 27

"So there's this really great guy. He is kind, considerate, loves Jesus, has great friends and a sense of humor. I really enjoy hanging out with him, but I'm not sure I have any interest beyond being his friend. However, he's made it clear to me that he is intentionally pursuing me and would like to take me out on a date. But I just don't know if I could like him in that way."

We've all been there. For some of us, this is our norm. At least it was for me. I was typically more interested in the guys who ignored me or just weren't romantically interested in me, and could never seem to conjure up an attraction for the guys who actually did pursue me. So what's a girl to do?

GIVE IT A LITTLE TIME.

My rule of thumb has always been to give a guy one to three dates. If a guy has the guts to ask you out, I think he deserves a chance. Obviously, there are exceptions to this. If you know something about him that is a legitimate deal breaker, fine, but generally I think we make up excuses rather than have legitimate reasons. I feel strongly about giving guys a chance, because way too many of us complain that guys don't ask girls out. So when they do, we need to respond positively. If we always shoot guys down, we are only reinforcing their fear. Let's encourage our single men to ask women out on dates!

AFTER A FEW DATES, ASSESS YOUR FEELINGS.

Do you enjoy spending time with him? Are you developing a friendship? Do you have things to talk about? Or do you dread when you see his name pop up on your phone? Would you rather be spending your time doing something else? I know this can be difficult, because a lot of times we feel conflicted or solidly neutral. If that's the case . . .

BE A STRAIGHT SHOOTER.

Tell him exactly what you are thinking or feeling. Don't mince words. If you enjoy hanging around him but don't feel any sort of attraction or romantic feelings toward him, tell him. Now, I've learned the hard way that most men will take that message as code for "Keep trying." You may be fine with that. Or, if you're like me, it will drive you crazy. So tell him that too. Be as honest and straightforward as possible. You are honoring him by being truthful. It may not feel like it, but it's the kindest thing you can do.

I know this may seem insultingly simple, but you shouldn't stress about it. Give him a chance, assess, and be honest. The best way to approach it is to consider *How can I treat him with as much respect as possible?* He deserves that.

Because my rule was one to three dates, I broke off a lot of early dating relationships. Sometimes it was mutual; many times it wasn't. Sometimes I did a great job of being kind, honest, and firm. Other times I did a horrible job. There are two times in particular that I look back on and still cringe. Want to know what's crazy? One of those was my husband! Seriously. We went out on three dates, and I knew I wasn't into him. It wasn't the worst way I'd ever dealt with the conversation, but at the end of date three when he made his intentions very clear, I just went along with it and agreed. I was a total chicken and couldn't tell him no to his face. Instead I sent him an email the next morning. An email! While I'm sure my email was very nice, he deserved better than that. I should have had the guts to tell him at the end of date three, when he was putting his own heart on the line, that my heart wasn't, in fact, on the table. And I'm still just so ashamed to tell that part of our story. Little did I know I could have given myself a better story to tell. Instead, someday I'll have to admit to my own children that I was a big, fat chicken who sent their dad an email to break up with him. Ugh!

RESIST THE TEMPTATION OF GOING DOWN THE "WHAT IF" PATH.

For example, *I don't think I like him, but what if this is the guy I'm supposed to marry?* Relationships are all about timing. I know too many stories of good friends who knew each other for more than six years before they were ready to date each other. And if there is one thing I learned from my own dating-to-marriage story, it's that God is totally and completely in control. If you keep your eyes on Him and genuinely want His best for your life, He'll work it all out. My husband and I were not ready for each other when we first dated. We both had some things to learn and there was some growth to be had in different areas of our lives before we were ready to walk down the aisle. Looking back, I see God's purpose in introducing us at that time, but it was another two years before we reconnected and began to date again. However, the first time around I definitely wasn't thinking I had broken things off with my future husband, and he wasn't thinking that either! So do not stress over this in your own dating life. You can make a decision based only on the information you have in the present. Trust God to take care of the future. Go with your gut right now and treat the guys you date with as much respect and kindness as possible.

I Can't Get over Him

Concern 28

> "I can't get over this guy. I've tried everything
> in the book to distract myself, and I've prayed,
> asking God to take the feelings away, but noth-
> ing changes."

Oh, sister. I've lived this one out too. More than a few times.
Whether we've been pining after a guy who doesn't know we're
alive or trying to get over someone after a breakup, we've all been
in that spot where we just wish we could control our heart and fix
our feelings.

I'm sorry to tell you, you can't. You simply cannot make yourself
get over someone or convince your heart to stop having feelings for
someone. Believe me, I've tried. Life sure would be easier if we
could, but God didn't design us that way.

So what do you do when you find your heart in this awful situation?

GO EASY ON YOURSELF.
Anytime I've been in this situation, I ended up getting really angry and annoyed with myself. I hated that I couldn't control my
emotions. I hated that I was so affected by another person. I felt
weak and ashamed. But you've got to give yourself a break. Your
heart is wired to fall in love (or "in like"). God created us for
intimate relationships. You are searching for an answer to fill a
God-given need that He placed in you. So don't be so hard on

yourself. It's okay for you to feel—even when it's unrequited love or breakup hurt.

CONTROL YOUR MIND.

Even though you can't control how you feel, you absolutely can control your thought life. Stop imagining him confessing his undying love for you. Stop imagining what it's going to be like when you get back together. Stop imagining your wedding. Seriously. STOP. You are full-on karate-chopping your heart when you let your imagination run rampant. When you catch yourself daydreaming, cut yourself off. Focus. Ask God to take those thoughts away. Ask Him to put new dreams in your head and heart.

KEEP PRAYING.

There was one time I spent nine months praying, BEGGING, God to take away my feelings for a guy. When that didn't work, I started praying that the guy would just ask me out. When that didn't work, I prayed that he would ask someone else out. When that didn't work...you get the idea. I prayed every possible outcome because I was desperate for change. I was so tired of liking a guy who didn't like me back and was anxious for God to change the situation. ANY change would suffice. The beauty that came out of those nine months is that I became incredibly dependent on the Lord. I was forced to cast my burden on Him daily, commune with Him, and rely on Him to give me the emotional strength to continue on. It sounds dramatic, but it really felt that way. So keep praying. God does not want you to walk through this alone. He wants you to trust Him and let Him do whatever it is He wants to do. He is delighted to carry your burden, and in time—God's perfect time—the situation will change.

You just have to let go and be okay with where you are. In time, your feelings will fade away. Author and psychologist Henry Cloud said, "Time does not heal all things, just ask an infected tooth. Time plus doing the right thing heals what hurts." It will take time, and it will take you controlling your mind, praying, and doing what you know you need to do to move on.

When I look back on those nine months, they were some of the most powerful, transformational months of my adult life. I learned to be fully dependent on God. I learned to be vulnerable with safe people. I learned to be okay with feeling weak and not in control. And the best part is that now I can look back and see the miraculous healing God performed on my heart. Healing so deep only He could do it.

So keep on marching, girl. There is light at the end of the tunnel. I promise. It will get better.

"So there's this guy. He keeps sending me mixed signals. We'll talk for a few hours (over text and calls) and then I won't hear from him for a while. He keeps making comments that lead me to believe that he likes me, but I'm not really sure. How can I tell if he likes me? How do I know if I like him?"

In college, I had a guy friend whom we'll call Sam. Sam was the king of mixed signals. At some points, I was positive he liked me. He called me, wanted to hang out, just the two of us, said things that sounded like code for "I like you as more than a friend," and so on. Then other times, he was totally MIA. I knew I didn't like him as more than a friend—maybe I was turned off by his wishy-washy behavior—but decided to ask a mutual guy friend for his opinion. While I wasn't sure Sam liked me, I didn't want to be leading him on. I asked my other friend—we'll call him Brad—if he thought I needed to confront Sam and find out what he was thinking.

Brad was stunned. While he agreed Sam was sending me mixed signals, he assured me I had zero responsibility in that game. If Sam wanted to come out and tell me he had feelings for me, then I needed to tell him I only wanted to be friends. But as far as Brad was concerned, it was Sam's own fault. He needed to step it up or walk away.

Even today, more than ten years later, I agree with Brad. If a guy likes a girl, he should make it clear. He needs to man up and tell you. If he likes you enough, he'll find the courage to do so. But if he is being inconsistent about it, it's not your responsibility to decipher what he's thinking. Plus, it's fairly difficult to read other people's minds. I don't know about you, but I've had very little success when trying to mind-read.

That said, don't be sending him mixed signals either. Don't flirt with him; don't constantly initiate text conversations and hangouts. If you're friends, that's great! Be friends. But don't treat him differently than any other guy friend you have.

If you're finding yourself trying to decipher your own feelings for him, my philosophy has always been that I don't need to decide if I like a guy until he decides to pursue me. Now, I am a compartmentalizing master and a don't-think-about-your-feelings ninja, so it's not hard for me to do that. But for the most part, I don't think we have to decide one way or another until the guy makes a move. It's like when you're interviewing for a job.

I used to labor and lament over whether or not I even wanted to apply for a job. One day, my dad finally looked at me and said, "You don't have to make a decision until an offer is on the table!" What a freeing thought. I didn't need to be sure I wanted to take the job when I applied for it. That's part of the process. You apply, have a few interviews, and get to know the company and the people, much like they get to know you. If they actually offer you the job, then and only then do you have a decision to make.

You could approach a lot of situations with this same philosophy. Dating included. You don't need to figure out whether you want to date a guy until he asks. Under most circumstances, say yes to a first date. Then after a date or two, you can make a better decision as to whether or not you want to continue to see where that relationship could go.

Of course, sometimes you just know. You know you're definitely not interested or you know you already think he's a total babe and would love for him to ask you out, but it doesn't always have to be that way. You don't have to make up your mind until after he asks you out. And you can say yes to a first, second, and third date until you decide one way or the other. You don't need to make up your mind before he makes his intentions clear. In fact, I think it's better if you don't.

Try not to worry about it. There's no need for you to decide if you have feelings for a guy if the homeboy hasn't actually stepped up and made his intentions clear. Truthfully, you probably can't really know if you're into him or not until he starts to be consistent in the way he treats you. Right now, you are confused because he is being confusing.

Should I Pursue Him?

Concern 30

"I recently went on a date with a guy I've had a little crush on for quite some time. Of course, after our date, my little crush turned into a big one. I know he's been interested for a while, but he has been slow to pursue me. What should I do? Should I pursue him?"

Unfortunately, you are growing up in a culture where it's rare that a guy knows how to pursue a girl. Most college guys are not men but, rather, boys who shave. So it's easy to end up in a flirty more-than-friends-but-undefined relationship, because guys don't know how to take the lead and treat a girl properly. But that doesn't mean that women should step it up and take the lead! In fact, you are doing him and yourself a disservice if you take the reins and pursue him.

In 2004, a book titled *He's Just Not That into You* took the single-girl culture by storm. You may have seen the movie, starring Jennifer Aniston, Bradley Cooper, Ben Affleck, Drew Barrymore, and Scarlett Johansson. It's a funny movie, based on a more hilarious book. Most if not all of the statements in the book are completely true, but if you ever get your hands on a copy, you'll realize how insane it sounds that an author actually needed to spell this stuff out for women.

My senior year of college, I lived in a house with five other girls, affectionately called the Wolfepack. No, this was not an ode to NC State with a spelling error. We lived on Wolfe Street, and some of my friends who'd lived there a few years earlier had coined the name. If you ever have a chance to live in an old, crummy house with five girlfriends, I highly recommend it. Some of my favorite memories happened in that house with those women.

One of the many quirky things we did as housemates was we kept a copy of *He's Just Not That into You* on our living room coffee table and would read excerpts out loud to one another as nighttime entertainment. Ninety percent of the statements in that book are just ridiculous. For example, something like, "If your boyfriend would rather smoke weed than hang out with you, he's just not that into you." That was my favorite.

We all see that and think, "Well, DUH!" but the truth is that we've all been in a situation where we like a guy more than he likes us, and we let him treat us like we are less than worthy.

If a guy isn't pursuing you, it's for one of two reasons: Either he is scared out of his mind, or he is just not that into you. Even if a guy is terrified of making a move, he should be so into you that he overcomes his fear in order to ask you out. You with me? I know this isn't exactly desirable news, because we want to be wanted and we want to convince ourselves that deep down he does want us. But listen to me, sister: You are lovely and worth wanting. However, not every boy is going to get that. And that's okay. Because your value and worth do not come from him wanting you.

So should you pursue him? My vote is heck no. Let him pursue you. Trust me on this. If he really wants to, he will. Now, before you go all *Sisterhood of the Traveling Pants* on me and accuse me of being old-fashioned, I am ALL for women being independent and being leaders. However, a crazy thing has happened in our culture: More women are going to college, more women are becoming college leaders, and more women are graduating from college, but we are seeing a decline in men's college graduation rates and campus leadership roles.

Am I saying that women need to stop excelling so that men can have a fighting chance? Absolutely not. You go do what you are fueled to do. You're being disobedient to God if you don't. Am I saying that we need to let men lead where, I believe, God has designed and intended for them to? You better believe it. If a guy pursues a girl and is the one leading the relationship, he is way more likely to be a leader as a husband and father—which our culture is greatly lacking. So, ladies, seriously, let him lead. Don't be the girl who has to drag the guy to the altar. You deserve better than that!

Sometimes, however, I think it's okay to give him a little nudge. I'm still not saying you should lead; we're talking about a nudge. There were several times in my dating past when I got tired of letting guys get away with being "Peter Pans," plagued with never-growing-up syndrome. I decided to give them a nudge, because I needed to know whether we were progressing toward dating or just remaining friends. And I'm all about being friends! But it gets hard for a girl to stay in limbo for too long. So if you're in a spot where it's time to give a nudge, here are the three things you should do.

1. WAIT TO SEE WHAT HE DOES.

Does he ask you on another date? Continue pursuing you? If the answer is no, you can just close the door right there. He's just not that into you.

2. WAIT SOME MORE.

Seriously. You need to give him room to pursue and lead. Perhaps he continues spending time with you but maybe isn't clear about his intentions or is sending mixed signals.

3. WHEN IT SEEMS LIKE YOUR TIME IS ALMOST UP AND YOU'VE WAITED AWHILE, CASUALLY SAY SOMETHING.

This does not mean that you plan a day and time to "confront" him. This does not mean that you write him an email or a letter. This does not mean that you send him a text saying, "So what's going on between us?" It means the next time you are hanging out, you bring up in a casual way, "So I love hanging with you, but sometimes I'm confused about whether we are just friends or maybe more than friends, and I'm curious what you're thinking…" That, ladies, is a nudge. It's a bold nudge, but all you're doing is asking a question and listening. You're not arguing your case. You're not trying to convince him to date you. You're not confessing your undying love. You are simply making sure he knows the ball is very much in his court.

But still let him lead! Even if you had to give him a nudge, set him up to lead. Trust me on this. As adults, men will default to passiveness and women will charge up to leadership, and it can cause all kinds of trouble in marriages and families. If he's not ready to lead you in a dating relationship, then he's not ready to date you. You deserve a guy who is going to act like a man, and he deserves to date a woman who encourages him to be a man.

I Fell into the "Friends with Benefits" Zone
Concern 31

> "A few months ago, I fell into the 'friends with benefits' zone with a guy, and now I've fallen for him. We spend all our time together, and when I bring up dating, he says he's not ready to commit. He says he needs more time to decide. I think I like him more than he likes me, and he's constantly sending me mixed signals. Should I stop pursuing him and tell him I don't want to be friends anymore?"

I hate these situations so much, and, sisters, it's becoming more and more common because of the hookup culture that is so prevalent in college today.

FIRST OF ALL...FRIENDS WITH BENEFITS?

UGH. It always, always leads to someone getting hurt. Women cannot be physically involved with someone, even couch-cuddling and hand-holding, without getting emotionally involved as well. Your brain, body, and heart aren't wired to operate independently. If you grow in deeper intimacy in one area, the others will follow. I cannot urge you enough to quit the FWB lifestyle. Make a commitment to yourself to never do it again. It's not worth it, and you deserve better.

AS THE OL' MOMMA SAYING GOES, "WHY BUY THE COW IF YOU CAN GET THE MILK FOR FREE?"

It's such a crass saying, but it's true. It sounds like this guy is already getting everything he wants from you without having to commit to being your boyfriend. He's getting his physical and emotional needs met, because y'all are basically acting like a couple. But he doesn't have to work for it or have any of the responsibilities that come with being in a committed relationship.

I didn't fall into the "friends with benefits" zone in the traditional way, but I found myself in several not-dating-but-clearly-more-than-friends relationships. We spent all our time together; he emotionally leaned on me, and I, on him. Everyone around us thought something was going on between us, but technically nothing was ever defined. Even though we weren't getting physical, I had still fallen into the trap of giving him some of the benefits of being in a relationship without any commitment on his part. I see a lot of college guys and girls do this. Be cautious of this! Either a guy should be just a friend or he should be your boyfriend (or someone you are dating). Don't give the goods away—even the emotional goods—without any commitment.

HE DOESN'T NEED MORE TIME TO DECIDE.

That's got to be one of the most classic lines men tell women to stall them. Please! By saying he needs more time, he's actually already made the decision to not date you. If he wanted to be in a committed relationship with you, if he wanted to introduce you as his girlfriend, he'd be doing it. "Need more time" is just a lame excuse he's using to avoid commitment.

The same goes for "It's just not the right time!" Yes, I believe timing is important, but if a guy is giving you any kind of a line about "time," you can be sure what he's really saying is, "I just don't want to." When you really want to be in a relationship with some-one, you make it work!

YOU SHOULD DEFINITELY STOP PURSUING HIM. (AHEM. READ CONCERN 30.)

That's his job. Yes, once you're in a committed relationship, there is more give-and-take. But until you are calling a guy your "boyfriend," he is the only one who needs to do the pursuing. Even once you're in a relationship, you're not pursuing him; you are en-couraging and cultivating the relationship.

YOU NEED TO CREATE AND COMMUNICATE VERY CLEAR BOUNDARIES.

You need to talk to him face-to-face and explain to him how you feel. Don't play games; just be honest. Tell him that you want to be in a dating relationship with him, but since that doesn't seem to be what he wants, you need to pull away and not be around him any-more. Set clear expectations and boundaries like, "I'm not going to avoid you, and certainly I will be kind if I run into you, but I need you to stop calling, texting, and contacting me. I need you to give me space. We can't be friends right now." Talk through specific sit-uations or scenarios you know will come up.

Now, I know you may go into this conversation with hope that he will say, "You're right.... Let's date," and sure, anything is pos-sible. But what's more likely is that he won't. So prepare yourself for that. Don't go into this conversation with false hope. Your goal should be to set boundaries and start protecting your heart. You are doing both of you a disservice by playing this friends-with-benefits game. By drawing clear boundaries, you are protecting your own heart and you're setting the bar higher and pushing him to become a better man.

CHAPTER SEVEN

Sex, Alcohol + the Party Scene
College Girl Concerns 32–39

> If you're spending your entire early 20s chasing the next party, what are you running away from?
> —Demi Lovato

> It would seem that Our Lord finds our desires not too strong, but too weak. We are half-hearted creatures, fooling about with drink and sex and ambition when infinite joy is offered us, like an ignorant child who wants to go on making mud pies in a slum because he cannot imagine what is meant by the offer of a holiday at the sea. We are far too easily pleased.
> —C. S. Lewis

We've all grown up with differing messages about whether sex outside of marriage is okay, or whether drinking underage or drinking at all is okay. You may have entered college with certain expectations of what the party scene would look like and whether or not you planned on engaging in it. Sometimes those predetermined plans change. Sometimes we are faced with an even harsher reality than we imagined.

It's important to evaluate what your parents and church taught you about these things, but even more important is for us to really look at Scripture and see what God has to say about them. Then the question becomes, do you trust that God is a good God, who really knows what's best for you? Or do you believe He is a boring God, who is just trying to control you with rules and regulations? How you answer those questions will determine how you engage with sex, drinking, and so many other lifestyle decisions.

We Keep Pushing Physical Boundaries More and More

Concern 32

> "I am completely planning on saving sex for marriage, but it's hard. My boyfriend and I keep pushing our boundaries. First it was really intense make-outs. Then hands started going everywhere, clothing has started to come off, and I won't go into more detail, but it's getting bad. Every time it happens, we talk about it afterward and swear we won't do it again, but it keeps happening. How do I get out of this cycle?"

BREAK UP WITH HIM. No, seriously. You might just need to break up with him. The reason I can say that so strongly is because that is part of my story. I was the one trapped within a cycle of shame and guilt. I desperately wanted out, but I didn't know how. We tried accountability partners, we tried setting up new rules and stricter boundaries, but we always found our way around them. Truthfully, deep down, I thought we would eventually get married and that would make everything okay. The shame and guilt would go away because he would be my husband, after all. If I broke up with him, it would never be redeemed or made right! At least, that's what I thought.

If I could cup my sweet, little twenty-year-old face in my now thirtysomething hands, I would say, emphatically, "Break up with him."

"It's easy for you to say that now," you protest.

You bet it is! I know now that God had something so much better for me. I know now that God wiped away the guilt and shame, that I learned I was not damaged goods but a beautiful girl who deserved to be—and would be—rightfully treasured.

At the time, I knew my boyfriend didn't have the same convictions I did. He wanted to save sex for marriage, but not because it was God's best for us; rather, he didn't want to get a girl pregnant or contract an STD. So all of the stuff that leads up to sex was "fine" for him. He didn't feel guilty or ashamed—that was all me. But what I know now is that since he didn't share my same convictions, he wasn't ever going to help me stay within what I believed to be appropriate physical boundaries. That should have shown me that we were not on the same page spiritually. Yes, he was a Christian, but he wasn't pursuing God's will for His life like I wanted to. And, ladies, there is no quicker way for you to become lazy in pursuing Christ or to wander off course from God's will than a cute boy who distracts you.

Now, that doesn't mean every couple who is struggling physically should absolutely break up. But I do know that once you start breaking the rules, it is almost impossible to quit crossing boundaries and pushing the limit even further.

If you are genuinely committed to each other and want to end the cycle of shame, you need to set up a system of accountability:

1. **Tell all of your roommates.** Hopefully, both of you have roommates who can help keep you accountable. Be honest with your struggles and ask them to help you. They can help by staying around when you are both home together. They can help by asking you every day, "How's it going?" They can help by calling you when it's late and you aren't home. Give them specific ways you want and need their support.

One of my roommates asked several of us to do this for her. We knew any night she was out with her boyfriend we had the invitation to call and check in on them. The call literally went like this:

Ring. Ring. Ring.

"Hello?"

"HAND CHECK!"

Sometimes she'd laugh and say, "Oh, we're totally fine. Just sitting here talking." Other times, "Uh, hiiiiiiiii." We knew, she knew, and that's all that needed to be said. "Do you guys need to come back over here?" we'd often offer. Sometimes they'd take us up on it and come hang out with the group. Sometimes they'd pull themselves together and be fine the rest of the evening. It's not a fail-safe plan, but there is something incredible about judgment-free accountability from people who love you and want to help you. I wish I had had the guts to ask for help when I was in my own too-hot-to-handle relationship.

2. **Tell someone who isn't a peer.** It's easy to confess to your friend or roommate, "Whoops! Screwed up again!" It's not as easy telling a mentor or someone you look up to. Hopefully, you have a campus minister, youth pastor, big sister, or someone else older than you who will really keep you accountable. Pick someone it would be hard to tell if you screw up. Again, you'll need to give them specific ways they can help keep you accountable. Let them invade your life.

3. **You and your boyfriend need to pray together about sexual purity.** My now-husband and I used to pray Romans 8:5–6: "For those who live according to the flesh have their outlook shaped by the things of the flesh, but those who live according to the Spirit have their outlook shaped by the things of the Spirit. For the outlook of the flesh is death, but the outlook of the Spirit is life and peace" (NET). Many evenings,

we would pray together, asking God to help us live according to the Spirit and not our flesh. Simply inviting God into our evening plans and asking Him to help us not tear off each other's clothes had a major impact. It reminded us both that we were in this together, and we both wanted to please God in our sexual behavior before and after marriage. It also invited God to influence our hearts and desires over and over and over—and we really needed that!

4. **Finally, if you genuinely love each other, you need to help stop each other when things are getting too intense** by saying, "I love you so much I'm stopping this." If you genuinely love each other, you want God's best for each other. And God's best is to strive for sexual purity as a couple. Too often, we take the message "We need to stop" in the moment of passion as rejection. But in a loving, God-honoring dating relationship, it's not rejection; it's a refocus: "Hey, let's love each other so well that we make each other look more like Jesus!" And while you're dating, that means stopping the passionate make-out sessions before they get out of control.

The fact that you're even grappling with this question is a great start! Pray earnestly, ask God to help you, and invite other people into the tension to help keep you accountable. You will never regret keeping your clothes on or choosing purity over passion. You will regret the times that you lose control. Take my word for it.

Do I Really Want to Save Sex for Marriage?

Concern 33

> "I was raised in a Christian home and in a church that preached that having sex before marriage is a sin. I understand that the Bible says that, but it seems outdated. What's so wrong with having sex if you're in a committed relationship with someone you love?"

I've had this conversation countless times with high school and college gals, and I get pretty heated about it, but probably not in the way you're thinking.

First, let me start by saying that, yes, I do think God's desire is for all of us to save sex for marriage. I believe He designed man and woman and also created sex. Obviously, one reason for sex was so humans could procreate, but He clearly designed it to feel good and to create connection between husband and wife. I believe that God's best version of sex—the way He intended it to be—is within the confines of a safe, loving, committed marriage.

Do you think God cares about your sex life? Do you think He might actually desire for you to have a great sex life? Maybe that's a weird question, but think about it. Is there any aspect of your life you think God doesn't care about? He cares about all of it, and He wants your life to be abundant—even your sex life. Humans did not invent sex (though our culture sure seems to act like we did). God did. So you better believe He cares about your sex life and wants you to have the fullness of His creation.

God has given us all kinds of experiences and gifts that He wants us to use and enjoy, but He also frequently gives us guidelines and rules surrounding them. This isn't to limit our fun or enjoyment but, rather, to protect us and help us experience His creation in the best possible way.

Too much of anything can turn into a bad thing, right? Alcohol, sex, relationships, money, success—all of those things are good, and God-given, but we all know of stories where those elements destroyed someone's life and family. Those gifts were taken outside the parameters God gave, and therefore abused, which eventually caused harm. Anytime we take God's gifts outside His parameters, it eventually causes us harm.

So, yes. I think if you want to experience God's best for you—even in your sex life—that means doing things His way. Save sex for marriage. Even if it doesn't fully make sense to you, can you trust that God's plan is better than your own?

If you and I were sitting across a table from each other, sipping on coffee, and you were truly grappling with this question, our conversation would take a quick turn. I wouldn't try to convince you to save sex for marriage by opening up the Bible. Instead, I'd ask you to tell me more about your relationship with Jesus.

I've learned over the years that when we find ourselves saying *I know the Bible says this, but...* or *I know God says this, but...* we have a much larger issue going on than we think. Instead of *Should I really save sex for marriage?* we should really be asking questions like:

- Do I trust God?
- Do I believe His plans are good for me?
- Do I want to know Him and please Him? Or do I want to be the god of my life?
- Who am I even living for—me or Him?

When we start to create our own rules for living, especially when they are in direct disobedience to God's plan, it's a bright-red flag that we have some much bigger spiritual issues at stake.

Look, I get it. I wanted to have sex before marriage too. And I struggled with it—big-time! But this is a heart issue, not a "my body, my rights" issue. If my relationship with Jesus is important, if there is depth in my love for Him, if I'm spending time in His Word and prayer, I'm going to struggle a lot less with issues like sex before marriage.

Now, here is where I actually get heated. I do not like the way most churches have communicated this to young women. When I grew up, I was told that my virginity was the best gift I could ever give away, so I should hold on to it in order to give it to my husband. We were given promise rings, and I was told to imagine exchanging promise rings with my husband at our wedding ceremony as part of our wedding vows. "True love waits" was one of the slogans I heard over and over, meaning that if it's real love—true love—you'll wait to have sex until marriage. Sadly, I think this message distorted God's intention for sex and the real motivation to save sex for marriage.

For one, if my virginity is the best gift I can give away, what happens if I'm not a virgin when I get married? My "best gift" has been wasted. Now, the first time you have sex with your husband—even if you two did wait until your wedding night—is cheapened. Your past sexual history has ruined everything. This is so wrong it kills me.

Sex is not an unforgivable sin. If you have sex before marriage and then later decide you want to save sex for marriage, that is amazing! If you and your fiancé wait to have sex until your wedding night, even if you both were sexually active before, I believe God is pleased! God doesn't judge us on our past sins every day. He has removed our sins from us as far as the east is from the west. He cares about our intentions, motivations, and desire to obey Him today.

Yesterday is forgotten. But the idea of *losing* your virginity or purity makes it sound like once you've had sex, it's over. You've ruined everything and have failed God.

Secondly, I don't like the idea of "giving away" your virginity as a gift. Sex is an expression of love. It's connection, it's intimacy, and it's fun. When my husband and I had sex for the first time on our wedding night, I didn't view it as "giving something away." I viewed it as a way to fully express my love to him and to fully receive his love for me. It wasn't a gift, and I didn't lose anything. It was a shared experience of connection, love, and gain!

I hope you will strongly consider God's plan and desire for you to save sex for marriage, even if you've already had sex before and now are wondering if you should wait from here on out. I do believe it is the best way. But I also believe there is always forgiveness and redemption. Keeping your virginity until marriage doesn't make God love you any more than He loves the girl who doesn't. Don't forget that—lest you become all high-and-mighty! But I do believe His plan is best, so the question remains: Can you trust that God's plan for sex is better than your own? Can you choose to put your relationship with the Creator of the Universe, your Savior, above a sexual relationship with someone who may or may not be your forever love? It takes a lot of faith and self-discipline, but I believe it's worth it.

Is It Okay to Drink?

Concern 34

> "My twenty-first birthday is coming up. I grew
> up in a home where alcohol was never present
> and I go to a very conservative church where
> the whole topic is taboo. I have friends who
> get drunk almost every weekend, and that's not
> what I want. I've never really had a desire to
> drink until recently. I guess because I know I
> can soon.... So what's okay?"

Maybe you grew up in a very conservative home where drinking alcohol was a no-no. While I think it is always important to obey and
honor your parents, I also believe that part of becoming an adult
is figuring out what you believe and how that impacts the way you
live, which might differ from your parents.

There are a lot of passages in the Bible that refer to alcohol.
Some positive, some negative.

> May God give you the dew of the sky and the richness of the
> earth, and plenty of grain and new wine. (Genesis 27:28 NET)

> Then you may spend the money however you wish for cattle,
> sheep, wine, beer, or whatever you desire. You and your
> household may eat there in the presence of the LORD your
> God and enjoy it. (Deuteronomy 14:26 NET)

He provides grass for the cattle, and crops for people to cultivate, so they can produce food from the ground, as well as wine that makes people feel so good, and so they can have oil to make their faces shine, as well as food that sustains people's lives. (Psalm 104:14–15 NET)

The LORD who commands armies will hold a banquet for all the nations on this mountain. At this banquet there will be plenty of meat and aged wine—tender meat and choicest wine. (Isaiah 25:6 NET)

Of course, wine was prevalent throughout the Jewish culture; it was part of every God-centered feast and celebration. In fact, the absence of wine was viewed as God's judgment!

Joy and gladness will disappear from the fruitful land of Moab. I will stop the flow of wine from the winepresses. No one will stomp on the grapes there and shout for joy. The shouts there will be shouts of soldiers, not the shouts of those making wine. (Jeremiah 48:33 NET)

The crops of the fields have been destroyed. The ground is in mourning because the grain has perished. The fresh wine has dried up; the olive oil languishes. (Joel 1:10 NET)

Perhaps even more interesting, Jesus' very first miracle was to turn water into wine (see John 2), and during the Last Supper, Jesus took the Passover tradition of wine to represent His blood and the new covenant (see Matthew 26, Mark 14, and Luke 22).

BUT WASN'T ALL OF THAT "WINE" REALLY JUST GRAPE JUICE?

I've heard churches teach that too, but unfortunately that's a pretty weak conclusion to make. There are also many verses in the Bible that prohibit drunkenness from wine. Now, correct me if I'm wrong, but I'm fairly sure you can't get drunk off of grape juice. So if the Jews and Jesus were only drinking grape juice, there would have been no need for those admonitions.

The grape juice theory also falls apart when we consider Jesus' miracle at the wedding in Cana (see John 2). When the jars of water, which Jesus turned into wine, came out to be served, the headwaiter said, "Everyone brings out the choice wine first and then the cheaper wine after the guests have had too much to drink; but you have saved the best till now" (John 2:10 NIV). The headwaiter is saying what every twenty-first-century host knows. You start the party with your nicest bottles of wine, then as the party goes on and folks drink all the good stuff, you can pull out the cheaper stuff. By that point, most folks will have had enough wine to dull the senses a bit! Again, that doesn't work if all we're serving is grape juice.

Finally, there's Luke 7:34: "The Son of Man has come eating and drinking, and you say, 'Look at him, a glutton and a drunk, a friend of tax collectors and sinners!'" (NET). This is Jesus Himself saying that He was being slandered for drinking alcohol. Again, people wouldn't have called Him a drunk if it was just grape juice.

BUT DOESN'T THE BIBLE SAY A LOT OF NEGATIVE STUFF ABOUT ALCOHOL TOO?

It definitely does.

Wine is a mocker and strong drink is a brawler; whoever goes astray by them is not wise. (Proverbs 20:1 NET)

Do not look on the wine when it is red, when it sparkles in the cup, when it goes down smoothly. Afterward it bites like a snake, and stings like a viper. (Proverbs 23:31–32 NET)

Those who get up early to drink beer are as good as dead, those who keep drinking long after dark until they are intoxicated with wine. (Isaiah 5:11 NET)

Those who are champions at drinking wine are as good as dead, who display great courage when mixing strong drinks. (Isaiah 5:22 NET)

And do not get drunk with wine, which is debauchery, but be filled by the Spirit. (Ephesians 5:18 NET)

Older women likewise are to exhibit behavior fitting for those who are holy, not slandering, not slaves to excessive drinking, but teaching what is good. (Titus 2:3 NET)

Depending on what Bible translation you're looking at, the word *wine* appears anywhere from 200 to 240 times. That's a lot of wine references! Some are positive, some are negative, and some are neutral. But none of those sides takes the majority. So what I have to take from that is there are positive, negative, and neutral components to alcohol and it's up to the individual person to decide how they want to respond.

Personally, I believe it's all about moderation. Scripture is really clear that drunkenness is a sin, but if you can have a few drinks and stay in control, it's up to you if you choose to partake on your twenty-first birthday or at any point in your adult life. Based on Scripture, it's clearly not wrong to have a drink or two to celebrate, but based on your upbringing and your church's convictions, or if alcoholism runs in your family, you may feel that the best decision for you is not to drink.

Let's get super practical for a moment.

If you decide to go out and drink on your birthday, my guess is that you'll need to set expectations with your friends ahead of time. Your big-drinker friends are going to want to pay for dozens of drinks to get you wasted. So you have to choose either to not celebrate with them or to make it really clear that you're not going to get crazy.

For girls who've never touched alcohol before, who are wanting to partake during the celebration of their twenty-first, I recommend one to two drinks max. A common rule of thumb is no more than one alcoholic beverage per hour. And you should always drink at least one glass of water for every alcoholic drink you have. Also, I feel the need to note that even following that "rule" does not mean you are safe to drive. My personal rule is I never drink more than one beverage if I am driving. It's just not worth the risk.

Again, if you just feel unsettled about drinking on your twenty-first, it's not worth it. No need to make yourself feel guilty or wonder if you made the right decision. But if you're wanting to celebrate your day with a drink or two, I think that is totally appropriate. It's also a great way to show your party friends that you can celebrate in moderation. But don't take my word for it. Take the time to be thoughtful about this. Spend a few moments reading over the Bible verses listed in this section. Let this be a time in your life where you allow God's Word to inform the direction of your decision.

How Do I Navigate the Party Scene?
Concern 35

Since I started at a small, Christian college, I didn't encounter the party scene much. I'm sure it was out there, but the trend at that school wasn't about house parties as much as it was about going downtown to all the bars. Since I didn't have a fake ID and wasn't interested in the bar scene, the whole thing was pretty much a non-issue for me.

But then I transferred to a large state university. And this wasn't just any school. Every year, when college rankings come out, my alma mater doesn't just show up on the lists for prettiest campus, best professors, and best food; it also frequently shows up on lists for the best parties! Seriously. Duke dogs (oh yes, that's our mascot) know how to party.

On top of that, I auditioned and made it into my school's premiere female a cappella group. If you're having visions of Anna Kendrick in *Pitch Perfect*, you're not far off. The a cappella community at my school was known for two things: having incredible voices and being incredibly hard partiers! They knew how to sing loud and how to throw down. And even though I wasn't into binge-drinking, I really wanted to be part of the whole community. As a transfer student, I was adamant about making an effort to plug in to my new surroundings and pursue people.

Maybe you're wondering about the same thing. As I've said before, it's important to say yes to social invites. That's how you meet people and make new friends. And while one-on-one lunches and coffees are great, there is something about Friday and Saturday nights that really seems to bond people. You could blame it on the drinking, but I think it also has to do with a combination of spending several hours together just hanging out and having fun. Getting to know people across a table is important; we have great discussions of depth when we do, but playing with people—hanging out, letting loose, goofing off—all of that is important too!

So if you're wanting to navigate the party scene without losing your marbles, here are a few tricks I came up with.

1. BYOB.

Now, it may seem obvious to bring drinks to a party, but I'm talking about nonalcoholic beverages. When I was in college, my BYOB of choice was Fresca. Fresca was basically the precursor to LaCroix—though, in my humble opinion, not as good! But I had never met an LC at that age, so I didn't know what I was missing. Fresca is light, fruity, no-cal, and caffeine-free. So I could nurse a six-pack of Fresca all night long and totally blend into the party scene, without people bugging me about getting a drink.

2. USE A KOOZIE.

If you're not from the South, you may have never heard of a drink Koozie. Let me introduce you to one of my very favorite things. A Koozie is a piece of insulated fabric or foam designed to wrap around your can or bottle and keep your beverage cold while keeping your hand dry. It's one of the best inventions of the twentieth century. You will never find me without a Koozie. I keep them in my house, car, and every purse I own; basically, I need access to a Koozie at all times. Of course, I love them for what they were designed for—to keep your beverage cool and your hand dry—but I found a particular love for them amidst the party scene. The hardest part for me when attending parties wasn't choosing to not get wasted but was repeatedly having to ward off my friends who desperately wanted me to drink with them. Using a Koozie to wrap around my Fresca didn't just give me a better Fresca experience; it kept my friends from hounding me when they could see I wasn't drinking a beer.

Now, if you're wanting to be obvious and take a stand that you're not drinking alcohol, then, by all means, don't use a Koozie. And I applaud you! I wasn't ashamed of not drinking, nor was I trying to fake that I was, but I just found the evening so much easier and more enjoyable if I didn't have people inspecting my beverage every few minutes. If anyone was really looking, they'd still see I was drinking Fresca. A Koozie doesn't hide the entire can. But typically, people weren't that observant and generally left me and my Fresca alone.

3. IF YOU'RE GOING TO PARTAKE IN A BEER OR TWO, YOU'VE GOT TO DECIDE AHEAD OF TIME AND YOU'VE GOT TO STICK TO YOUR NUMBER.

Personally, drinking wasn't this huge intrigue. I had grown up in a household where drinking in moderation was acceptable, and occasionally my parents would let me have a glass of wine with them during dinner. But I didn't really like beer or hard liquor, and wine wasn't often served at these house parties, so prior to turning twenty-one, I had no issue with staying completely clear of alcohol at parties. Once I turned twenty-one, however, I began to acquire a taste for beer and other cocktails, so while I still brought my six-pack of Fresca, I would occasionally have a few drinks. The trick I learned to this was determining my number ahead of time and sticking to that number. I usually chose a number between one and three, and if more than one, I would space the drinks out over the evening, alternating my Frescas in between. The nights I didn't choose a number beforehand, I often overdrank. It's too easy after having a couple of drinks to just keep drinking, because you feel so nice and loose. After those evenings, I'd wake up the next morning with a bad headache and a guilty conscience. But the point is, if you don't start the night with a plan, you'll often fall prey to the whims of the evening or even someone else's plan.

The choice is up to you. You don't have to navigate the party scene at all if you'd rather just skip it altogether. I just felt strongly about being part of the community I was placed in and being a light in dark places. You have to have strong resolve if you're going to be a bright light in dark corners, but I think that's what Jesus modeled for us. So be wise, pray about it, but go ahead and navigate that party scene if you think you can do it without losing your brightness!

What's All This Talk About Sexual Assault and Rape?
Concern 36

"My college made us watch these sexual assault tutorials as part of our orientation, but is that really a thing I need to be worried about?"

This is one of those conversations where I always find myself putting on my "mom" hat. I know those videos seem ridiculous, and the thought of being sexually assaulted or raped seems unlikely, but it hurts my heart to say it's not uncommon. Working on a college campus for more than ten years as an RA, a hall director, a student organization advisor, a member of a crisis response team, a trained volunteer for a sexual assault hotline, and even just because I was known as someone who cared and would help, I have been told about so many sexual assaults I've lost count.

I've sat with survivors and processed, years after their assault happened and also just hours later. I have heard from both men and women who were raped or sexually assaulted. I have gone to a young woman's dorm room and helped her bundle up her clothes, the bedsheets, anything with evidence on it, wrapping them in a pillowcase so that she could have them tested. I have escorted women to the hospital and waited for them while they had a rape kit exam. The stories I know, the hurts I've hugged, they still break my heart to this day.

Sexual assault doesn't just mean *rape*. Sexual assault is any unwanted sexual contact or behavior. If a guy gets handsy with you at a party and you didn't give consent, even that is sexual assault.

*   *   *

So, yes, it's real. Do I want you to *worry* about it? No, but I want you to be very aware, very careful, and I want you to watch out for your friends like a hawk.

Between 20 and 25 percent of college women will be sexually assaulted. That's one in every four or five women. At least 50 percent of college sexual assaults involve alcohol. But 90 percent of acquaintance rapes (or what you may know as "date rape") involve alcohol.[1] And perhaps the most horrifying statistics of all: Fraternity brothers are three times more likely to rape than other college men,[2] and sorority women are 74 percent more likely to experience rape than other college women.[3] Of course, that doesn't mean fraternity guys are bad dudes, but it signifies that sexual assaults often happen at large parties with excessive drinking and drug use. Rape or sexual assault is rarely a stranger jumping out from behind a bush. It's usually someone you know, are at a party with, or even go on a date with.

I tell you this not to scare you but to state reality. Anecdotally, out of the numerous accounts shared with me, I can't remember a story that didn't involve alcohol in some way. Of course, it is never the survivors' fault, even if they were drinking. Yet the bleak reality is that if you are binge-drinking, you are at risk. I also know women who didn't drink too much, but unfortunately a guy slipped something into their drink—a roofie, GHB, or another "date rape drug." Of course, these women could have been drinking club soda and still would have been susceptible to a perpetrator.

The point to all of this is that you have to stay aware in order to be safe. Here are a few rules I abide by and encourage my friends and students to do the same:

- Avoid drugs and excessive use of alcohol. Be careful. Really watch how much you drink and don't go overboard.
- Trust your instincts. If you feel uncomfortable, get out of the situation. No matter how awkward it may be. Your safety is more important.
- Don't ever accept a drink that you didn't pour yourself. It's too easy for a guy to pour you a drink and slip something into it. When in doubt, don't drink it. It's not worth it.
- Watch your drink at all times. If you set it down, consider it gone. Simply covering it with a napkin does nothing.
- Talk about this ahead of time with your girlfriends. Come up with your own rules and be one another's security.
- Don't ever leave a girl alone. Girls who go to parties together need to stay together.
- Utilize your trusted male friends as allies as well.

This list is by no means exhaustive. My hope is that it gets you thinking and that you become more aware of your surroundings and decisions when in high-risk situations.

Other Resources

Florida Institute of Technology Student Counseling Center
    www.fit.edu/caps/documents/daterape.pdf
RAINN (Rape, Abuse & Incest National Network)
    www.rainn.org/statistics/campus-sexual-violence

Recovering from Sexual Assault

Concern 37

"What are my options if I've been raped or sexually assaulted?"

I am so sorry. I hate the broken, evil parts of this world that make
this a common conversation. If you have been raped or sexually assaulted in any way, you have several options and resources to help
and support you.

YOU CAN TELL SOMEONE IN CONFIDENCE.

I know this is a terrifying step, but I hope you will take it. Healing
from a sexual assault is a process that takes time, but you don't
have to do it alone. Tell someone who is safe, someone you trust.
Maybe you start with a best friend, and then if you decide you
want to take action, she can go with you when you report it to
someone official. Or maybe you'd rather call an anonymous hotline
or speak with someone else, like a therapist, who can guide you
through your resources. Whatever feels most comfortable to you, I
pray you'll tell someone.

If you tell someone who works for your university, there is a
difference between who can keep your story confidential and who
is required to report it. If you tell a licensed counselor or therapist, a medical provider, or oftentimes the university chaplain or
clergy, you would be covered under confidentiality. Some schools
have an advocate for sexual assault survivors, who is also a confidential resource. Folks in those roles won't report anything you

tell them unless it is clear that your life or someone else's life is in danger. However, most other university employees are required by law to report any notification of sexual assault. So if you are unsure whether or not you want to report your experience, it can be best to start with a confidential resource.

Of course, you can also tell your best friend or roommate. Just be aware that if she is also an RA on campus (even if she isn't *your* RA) or serves in any kind of capacity where she assists in maintaining the safety of students on campus, she is probably required to report it as well.

You can also talk to a trained specialist by calling RAINN's National Sexual Assault Hotline at 800-656-HOPE (4673) or by starting a confidential online chat at https://hotline.rainn.org/online. RAINN can give you resources while you maintain your anonymity. Your university may also have an anonymous hotline.

YOU CAN RECEIVE MEDICAL ATTENTION.

If the assault happened within the last seventy-two hours, you can go to a medical facility, where professional staff not only will care for your body but also will collect DNA evidence. This is called a sexual assault forensic exam, or a "rape kit." What a rape kit does is it allows you to have evidence collected from your body and clothes in case you decide to press charges. Getting a sexual assault forensic exam does not mean you have to report the assault or press charges. It just gives you the option to do so. In fact, you don't have to decide that night or even for several months. Each state differs on how long it will keep your kit evidence, but most keep an unreported kit for six months. Remember, you don't have to do this, but it keeps the door open if you later decide you want to report the assault and press charges. However, not just any hospital or medical facility can conduct a sexual assault forensic exam; it has to have an employee with professional certification as a sexual assault nurse examiner (also known as SANE certification). A quick call to RAINN (800-656-HOPE [4673]) or your university hotline would give you a listing of where to go in your area.

YOU CAN REPORT IT TO LAW ENFORCEMENT.

You can do this through a few channels. You can call 911 and report the assault to the police. If the assailant goes to your college, you can report it to the university. You can do both. When I personally counseled women who wanted to report, I typically encouraged them to start at the university level. It's not quite as jarring a process, and you are usually working with folks who have been highly trained to help sexual assault survivors. However, the university can only do so much. They can make sure you aren't in any classes together, or remove you from a dorm if you live in the same vicinity as the assailant. Ultimately, they will take him or her through the judicial process, which could result in suspension or expulsion. However, if you are looking for justice beyond a school sanction, you'll need to involve the local police. Most times, university staff can help you navigate that system as well. They often have relationships with local police and will know the best person to call. During my time working at a university in Washington, DC, I had specific campus officers and city police officers whom I implicitly trusted and would request when dealing with a sensitive situation.

As I mentioned earlier, most university employees are required by law to report any notice of sexual assault. That includes RAs, hall directors, professors, and almost any other faculty or staff. They will do their best to care for you and protect you, but they have a legal obligation to tell the university, to keep others safe, and to make sure that all students are held responsible for their actions. So share only with someone in a university role whom you trust to help you navigate the university reporting process.

By law, your college campus has to have someone on staff who serves as the Title IX coordinator. That person's job is to respond to any form of sex discrimination on campus. You may have heard about Title IX in reference to women's athletics, but it also includes regulations about sexual harassment and any form of discrimination based on gender. If you decide to report your experience to a university official, the Title IX coordinator is usually an easy person to identify with a quick search on your school's website.

IF YOU ARE READING THIS BECAUSE A FRIEND CAME TO YOU AND TOLD YOU ABOUT HER EXPERIENCE BEING SEXUALLY ASSAULTED:

- Tell her you are so sorry this has happened to her.
- Remind her that this was not her fault.
- Tell her you believe her.
- Tell her you will support her however she wants.
- You don't need to bombard her with questions. You don't need all the details. You just need to be willing to listen to whatever she wants to share. The two best questions to ask are "Are you okay?" and "Can I help you?" Let her tell you what she wants to tell you from there.
- Ask her if she wants to seek medical attention or report it. Don't push. This is her choice. She needs to be in control. If she is open to either of those things, offer to go along with her.
- Continue to support her. Healing from a sexual assault isn't a ten-step plan, nor is it resolved within a few weeks or months. Keep reaching out, checking in, and reminding her you are there for her.

The easiest resource to reach out to is RAINN: 800-656-HOPE (4673). Their staff can walk you through all of your options and tell you where to go or whom to reach out to for local help. If you're reading this section proactively, take a minute and find out what your school's resources are. A quick internet search will probably do the trick, but if not, ask your RA! On the campus resources form that follows, write down the university hotline, the name and email address of the campus advocate for survivors of sexual assault, the Title IX coordinator's name and email address, and any other resource that could be helpful. Then you'll always know where it is and can easily flip to it if the need ever arises.

Your Campus Resources

Does your university have a sexual assault hotline? If so, write the phone number here:

_____

Does your university have an advocate for sexual assault survivors who will maintain confidentiality? If so, write the name and email / phone number here:

_____

Who is your school's Title IX coordinator? Name and email / phone number:

_____

Where is your university counseling center? Address, email, and phone number:

_____

Any other important resources?

_____

_____

_____

_____

I know it may feel like you're all alone in this, but there is someone who has been with you every step of the way and who knows exactly what you're feeling. I have a dear family friend who suffers from extreme pain due to multiple sclerosis. She often remarks that on her worst days, lying in bed in the dark when any sound, light, or touch is unbearable, she has only three things: herself, pain, and God. Even in your darkest days, He is with you. He has never left you and He never will. Talk to Him. Cling to Him. He is the safest place for you to lay down your pain and hurts.

> You keep track of all my sorrows. You have collected all my tears in your bottle. You have recorded each one in your book. (Psalm 56:8 NLT)

> The LORD is a shelter for the oppressed, a refuge in times of trouble. (Psalm 9:9 NLT)

Other Resources

Forensics for Survivors
    www.surviverape.org/forensics/sexual-assault-forensics/answers
    -to-faq
RAINN (Rape, Abuse & Incest National Network)
    www.rainn.org
"Talking to Victims," TEDxSpokane talk by W. Scott Lewis
    https://youtu.be/5x0ypp5REaU

I Think Something Is Really Wrong with Me

Concern 38

"Recently I've found myself getting overwhelmed with anxiety. Sometimes it gets so bad I start to hyperventilate. It literally feels like an elephant is sitting on my chest and I can't get enough air. I've even blacked out a few times. Am I having panic attacks?"

"I get that college is a major change and it takes time to fully transition, but I'm not just homesick or unhappy.... It's much worse. Do you think I'm depressed?"

"I've never been an emotional person before, but lately I find myself getting angry. The weirdest thing will set me off, and I will completely lose it, like I'm seeing red. Is that normal?"

Maybe you're experiencing something that sounds a lot like one of those scenarios. Or maybe you're experiencing something completely different, but you're still wondering if something might be wrong with you. Let me just say this:

If you are at all wondering if something is off with your mental or emotional health, go talk to a professional! I'm not saying you have to commit to a year of therapy. I'm saying go see a counselor one time, give them a brief synopsis of what's going on with you, and see what they think. There is a counseling center just for you on your college campus. It is probably free. If it's not free, it's likely based on a sliding scale, which means you can afford it. If you don't want to ask Mom or Dad to pay for it, tell the counseling center that, and they will give you the best deal they can—I'm talking like twenty-five dollars.

If you had a rash on your body for a few weeks, which was constantly itching and driving you crazy, wouldn't you go see a doctor to have it checked out? I sure hope you would! The same should be true for your mental and emotional health. If something is going on in your head or heart that's impacting your day-to-day routine, that should be a red flag.

And what do you have to lose? An hour of your time and maybe twenty-five dollars. But you have everything to gain. Free, or very cheap, counseling and the opportunity to figure out what's going on with you and how to become a healthier version of yourself—the woman God designed you to be!

Here's the science on this kind of thing. There is so much going on in your brain during this time of life, and I don't just mean what you're thinking about! Your brain is in the process of final development. Research shows that your brain isn't fully developed until the age of twenty-five. So right now, that globby substance in between your ears is working really hard to fully form. The prefrontal cortex, which is the part of your brain that is currently stitching itself together, influences a lot of things—like your attention span, complex planning, decision making, impulse control, logical and organized thinking, personality development, and risk management. No wonder your brain is doing some wackadoodle things! Combine that with a new environment and a lack of community— or at least a lack of relationships that go further back than a couple of years—and it's no wonder some things are getting unbalanced in your head or heart.

Meanwhile, studies show that some things can hurt the final development of your prefrontal cortex—like chronic stress, alcohol abuse, drug abuse, poor diet, relationship troubles, sleep problems, and social isolation.[4] Hello! Does that sound like college?!

Of course, this doesn't mean that by going to college you're hurting your brain or it won't properly develop. You have to remember that God is in control of all things—including your brain function. However, it points to some strong reasons as to why you may be having a harder time coping with anxiety or feelings of sadness, depression, or even anger.

Studies also show that most mental health conditions appear for the first time during the ages of eighteen to twenty-four.[5] That doesn't mean you are going to fight a lifelong mental health condition; it just means it's common for those kinds of things to pop up during this season of life. A 2004 study conducted by the National Alliance on Mental Illness reported that 50 percent of college students rated their mental health below average or poor. Thirty percent reported problems with schoolwork due to mental health, and one in three students reported prolonged periods of depression.[6] And those are just the ones who reported it! Another survey, from 2013, found that 57 percent of college women reported experiencing episodes of extreme anxiety.

I could go on and on, but I'm not trying to overwhelm you with statistics. I'm trying to help you see that if you are experiencing these things, you are not alone. However, as my friend who is the momma of one college graduate, one current college girl, and a high school boy puts it: "It's not uncommon, but it's not normal."

What you're experiencing may be common, but it's not normal—meaning it's not okay. A huge part of college is learning to take care of yourself, and that includes your mental, emotional, and spiritual health! Go talk to someone. Make an appointment at your college counseling center. Reach out to someone older and wiser who really knows Jesus and share with them what's been going on. If you don't know anyone like that, reach out to a staff member of a campus ministry or church. Just reach out to someone.

The worst thing you can do is just ignore whatever is going on with you. The best thing you can do is lean into it. Figure out what's going on in your head and heart, and talk through it. I have gone to counseling during several different seasons of my life. Each time, I needed an outsider's objective opinion on what was going on with me. Sometimes they were Christian counselors; other times they weren't. But every time, it allowed me to unpack some unhealthy thoughts and patterns I was holding on to and take them to God. I needed the help of a professional counselor, family and friends, and especially Jesus. We all do!

Cast all your anxiety on him because he cares for you. (1 Peter 5:7 NIV)

Other Resources

"Depression and Anxiety Among College Students" by Margarita Tarakovsky, Psych Central
    https://psychcentral.com/lib/depression-and-anxiety-amongcollege-students/
"Anxiety and Depression" by Joel Brown, BU Today
    http://www.bu.edu/today/2016/college-students-anxiety-and-depression/

My Friend Told Me She's Thought About Hurting Herself

Concern 39

> "My friend recently confided in me that sometimes she thinks about ending her life. I'm really scared for her and want to help her, but I'm not sure how to do that without breaking her trust."

Another really heavy part of one of my past jobs was that if a student reported thoughts of suicide—to a friend, or an RA, or even if they had posted something suspicious on social media—I would be called in to meet them in their dorm room to ascertain if they were safe enough to be left alone or if they needed to be hospitalized. It sounds dramatic, but if someone has had real thoughts about hurting themselves in a way that would jeopardize their life, the last thing we want to do is leave them alone to take action.

Oftentimes, a friend won't come straight out and tell you they are having suicidal thoughts, but they may try to open up to you in another way. They may tell you how depressed they are or tell you of a current situation in their life that is making them wonder if life is worth living. They may even ask you if you have ever thought about taking your own life. If you ever find yourself in a conversation that seems to tip its hand toward suicidal thoughts, be bold and ask this question: "Have you thought about hurting yourself?" If their answer sounds anything remotely like a yes, dig a little deeper. I find the simple words "Tell me" or "What have you thought about?" usually open the door.

Here's the thing about suicidal thoughts. If someone is really thinking about it, you have to tell a professional. I know this seems like a horrible breach of trust, but you can't be the only person on the planet who knows that your friend has thought about killing themselves. That is too much weight on you, and it's also not what's best for your friend.

If a friend tells you that they have recently thought about hurting themselves, respond with love, ask questions, listen, and then tell them, "Your life matters. You are loved and valuable. I care about you so much and would be so upset if you ever did anything to hurt yourself that we have to tell someone else who can help you." Use the word *we*. *We* have to tell someone else.

Your friend may push back or even appear angry, but you have to remember that deep down she told you because she wants help. She doesn't want to keep this secret any longer, and while she may have thought her secret would stop with you, that is not what's best for her or you. *We* (you both) need help.

Hopefully, she'll be open to telling someone else with you, but if she's not, you'll have to explain to her that you are still going to reach out to someone who will be better equipped to help her.

If you're living on campus, you can always start with your RA or hall director. Both have been trained on how to respond to students experiencing suicidal thoughts, and both know the proper resources to refer your friend to. You could also call your campus counseling center or the National Suicide Prevention Lifeline at 1-800-273-TALK (8255). There is also a Crisis Text Line; simply text "START" to 741741. Of course, if you have the option to tell someone locally, who can be there face-to-face, I highly suggest that. However, sometimes calling an anonymous line seems like the easiest first step. If that makes your friend feel the most comfortable, then start there.

*   *   *

If you are ever in a situation where you think your friend is going to hurt herself that very moment, you have to call the police or campus security. While that may seem like a strange response, if someone is truly threatening to end their life, the best thing you can do is have someone arrive on scene who will immediately get them to safety. There were several times I had to call campus police to intervene when I was afraid for a student's life. It feels horrible in the moment, but it's always the right decision if you are preventing someone from taking their own life.

Whether you or your friend are having suicidal thoughts, I can't stress enough how loved you are and how valuable your life is. God uniquely designed you and created you for a purpose. He has great plans for you. I know that may be hard to believe in this moment, but I pray you will believe me. You matter. You matter to the Creator of the Universe. He loves you. He's crazy about you, and He is with you right now. Talk to Him. Ask Him for help. And then reach out to a professional who can get you the help you need.

He heals the brokenhearted and binds up their wounds. (Psalm 147:3 NIV)

May your unfailing love be my comfort, according to your promise to your servant. (Psalm 119:76 NIV)

CHAPTER EIGHT

Jesus, Take the Wheel

College Girl Concerns 40-46

God never said the journey of this life would
be easy, but He did say that the arrival would
be worth it.

—Max Lucado

Just a few years into my career working with college students, I
began to see a pattern of sophomores and juniors completely walking away from the Christian faith they had been raised to believe.
These were students I knew well, students who sat in my office and
discussed elements of faith, shared their doubts, struggled with the
tensions of what they had been taught and what they now faced in
college. During our many conversations, I never worried that they
would reject their Christian beliefs. I saw their struggles and con-
templations as normal seasons of doubt, which would inevitably
result in a fresh commitment to Jesus and a deeper faith in His
promises. I was wrong.

Of course, not all students who doubt or struggle with their
Christian beliefs will walk away from their faith, but more and
more studies are showing that it is a frequent occurrence.[1] Perhaps
some students never owned their faith to begin with. They may
have been raised in a Christian home and may have grown up attending church, but maybe it never connected with their head and
heart. For others, I think they believed the gospel and when they

were surrounded by a community of believers, it was easy. But once in college—and surrounded by a community of friends who didn't share the same beliefs—questions and doubts crept in that they didn't have answers to. The questions and doubts aren't the problem. It's when your beliefs aren't anchored to a foundation of solid truth and knowledge. If you can't articulate why you believe what you believe, when the questions and doubts come—and they will come—you have nothing to stand on.

Jesus' brother James wrote a rather startling letter to the church. One of the verses I've always had a hard time wrapping my head around says, "If any of you lacks wisdom, you should ask God, who gives generously to all without finding fault, and it will be given to you. But when you ask, you must believe and not doubt, because the one who doubts is like a wave of the sea, blown and tossed by the wind" (James 1:5–6 NIV). The latter part of that verse is one of the many reasons I find James' letter startling. How can we be expected not to have occasional doubts? Isn't that part of being human?

I can't think about doubting, and waves of the sea, without a man named Peter coming to mind. Peter was one of Jesus' closest friends. He was one of the twelve apostles, and he always displayed a fierce loyalty to and love for Jesus. One spectacular evening, the twelve apostles are in a boat crossing the Sea of Galilee while Jesus chose to stay behind on land. Later that evening, Jesus decides to take a casual stroll across the sea, perhaps not even planning to get into the boat, but simply to meet His friends on the other side. However, when the apostles see Him, they are terrified. Wouldn't you be? They had never seen a man, much less Jesus, walk on water. To them, the only logical conclusion is that a ghost is approaching their boat. Yet after Jesus assures them that it's okay— "It's just Me, guys!"—Peter excitedly responds, "Lord, if it's you, tell me to come to you on the water." That doesn't sound like doubt to me. It sounds like incredible faith, actually! Yet you probably know the story too well. Peter climbs out of the boat, starts walking on water, and begins to take in his surroundings: the wind, the waves, the darkness. He panics and begins to sink. "Jesus, save me!" he cries. And how does Christ respond? He reaches out His hand, saves him, and whispers, "You of little faith...why did you doubt?" (See Matthew 14:22–31.)

So Peter had this incredible faith, but then he got scared and overwhelmed by his circumstances and doubts, which led to his sinking. Yet did he drown? No! Because Jesus was right there, holding out His hand, and Peter grabbed it. In my glorified imagination, that's what it looks like when we doubt but choose to grab on to the truth of the gospel. If we know why we believe what we believe, if we can articulate the conviction that we have, it's as easy as reaching up and grabbing hold of The Hand that is waiting for us to latch on to. It's when we don't have a good foundation of truth that when we start to drown, we don't even see Jesus' hand reaching out for us. The lifesaver is there; we just have to know where to look.

You may have had seasons of doubt or trials when you were in high school. Two of the greatest seasons of doubt in my entire life were in middle school and high school. Even still, college will likely test your faith more than anything you've experienced so far. The testing, doubts, and questions aren't bad. It's what you do with them that matters. The key to Christian growth is God's Word, God's Spirit, and God's people. To be grounded in the truth, you have to press in. You have to spend time reading the Bible, you have to learn how to listen to and submit to God's Spirit, and you have to surround yourself with fellow believers. That doesn't mean you can have friends only in the Christian community—far from it! But you need friends you can turn to during seasons of doubt who will encourage you, challenge you, and always point you back to The Hand reaching out to you.

However, it's up to you. Your faith can no longer be your parents' faith or your church's faith; it must become your own. College is a great time to explore what your parents and church raised you to believe. As hard as it may seem, your parents and your church may not be correct about everything they taught you. Now is the beginning of your journey to figure it out for yourself! *What does the Bible say about how I ought to live my life today? What is the gospel? What did Jesus save me from and what did He save me for?* Jesus' hand is reaching out to you. He is ready to walk alongside you through this journey. Will you grab hold of Him and follow?

How Do I Pick a Church?
Concern 40

"I grew up in the same church my whole life,
and now that I have to choose my own church,
I realize I have no clue how to go about it.
There are so many churches to choose from.
How do I pick a good one?"

This book is filled with advice that I hope you will consider and even apply. While I obviously feel strongly about everything written in these pages, there is one thing I am especially adamant about: I beg of you, please pick a church and faithfully attend every week while you're in college.

I know it's often the last thing you want to do on a Sunday morning when you also have the options of sleeping in, brunching with friends, or homework time, but if you are at all serious about pursuing your walk with Christ, you need to get your butt in a pew on Sunday morning. If you attend a weekly campus ministry gathering or even a college small group, that is wonderful. And I hope you do those things. But I still can't urge you enough to commit to a local church, show up, and even get involved!

Truthfully, I really struggled to do this. My freshman year, I hopped from church to church for the entire fall semester. Then in January, I finally found a church to stick with for the rest of the school year, but I only showed up for the hour-and-fifteen-minute service on Sunday mornings, without speaking to a soul other than the friends I drove there with. After I transferred, I had a horrible time finding another church I liked. Every church I visited was so different from the church I was raised in. I couldn't find one that fit me. Eventually, I chose the church most of my friends attended. I stuck with it, but I never got involved. I would slide in halfway through the worship set (because I thought the music was horrible) and duck out the second the service was over. And that's just not what church is supposed to be about. Here's what I wished someone had pushed me to consider:

DO YOU WANT TO EXPLORE DENOMINATIONS?

Some of you don't even know what a denomination really is. Others of you may be horrified that I suggest this. I grew up in a nondenominational Bible church. So I didn't really know what the big deal was. I attended a Baptist church and then a Presbyterian church during college. You may find you really enjoy a certain denomination that you have never been exposed to, or maybe you strongly prefer the denomination you were raised in. Either way, if you're interested, I encourage you to explore and see what else is out there. Don't let your exploration look like mine, where I rejected every church that was different. Allow it to open your eyes to other ways that believers worship and connect to God. I like to imagine how we'll all be together in heaven someday, worshipping together. The Charismatics, the Anglicans, the Methodists, the Baptists, the rock bands, the choirs, the gospel singers, the organists—we will all be together worshipping in one accord! Remember, God sees the heart—He doesn't care about the style or the wrong notes or have a genre preference. I think we each need to ask God to give us a true worshipper's heart, and to worry less about the style and the sound.

DO YOUR RESEARCH.

When exploring denominations and churches, you need to do your homework. Find out what a church believes. What is their doctrine? Is their teaching biblical? You need to be confident in what your church stands for and what is being preached there on a regular basis. My best advice is to find a church that opens up the Bible, reads from it, and teaches the passage that's been read. That may seem obvious, but there are a lot of churches that don't do that these days. If your church isn't teaching straight from the Bible, you may just be getting a feel-good personal-growth message. There are a lot of self-help books out there where you can get that kind of stuff, but you should be fed truth straight from the Bible when you go to church.

DECIDE ON TWO OR THREE TRAITS YOU WANT YOUR CHURCH TO EXHIBIT.

My top three traits were biblical teaching, good worship music, and a multigenerational church. However, in college, I had to pick a church that had two out of those three. At the end of the day, I had to let go of the standards I was demanding of the worship band. I once heard a preacher say, "God did not give you the spiritual gift of criticism." Ouch! Are wisdom and discernment spiritual gifts? Absolutely. Criticism? I don't think so. Yet I find so many Christians—including myself—are so critical of the way their church does things. If you're finding a critical spirit pop out of you, ask God to help. Ask for forgiveness for being so critical of His sons and daughters, whom He loves and who are working so hard to please Him. Ask Him to give you His eyes and perspective to see His church.

Many times, Christians have a list of eight or nine traits they want a church to exhibit. The problem is that there is not a church on this planet that is perfect or that has been crafted exactly for you. That was a huge part of my church-shopping problem. I was looking for a church that met my laundry list of needs and wants. However, church isn't really about *you*. It's about finding a church that teaches truth, that allows you to be connected with other believers, and where you can worship our Savior.

WHEN VISITING A CHURCH, ATTEND THREE OR FOUR CONSECUTIVE SUNDAYS.

It's really hard to judge a church from a one-time experience. You should go consistently for a few weeks to get the overall feel.

WHEN YOU FINALLY DO CHOOSE A CHURCH—AND YOU DO HAVE TO CHOOSE BEFORE TOO LONG—GET IN THERE AND SERVE.

Join a Sunday school or a small group. Serve in the nursery, children's ministry, youth group, or worship band, or be a greeter. Just do something. The point of church is not for you to show up for an hour each Sunday. It is for you to get involved, to know other believers in your community, and to serve. I didn't do this in college, because I was so involved in my school's InterVarsity ministry. I saw that as community. While that's all fine and good, I missed out on serving others younger and older than I was. I also didn't get to experience being part of a larger, more diverse body of believers. It's too easy to surround yourself only with peers during college, and I think we sell ourselves short when we aren't part of the bigger picture of God's family. So get involved and love on people younger than you and seek out older folks to share their wisdom and experience with you.

That's why I believe it's so vital for college men and women to plug into a local church. You need the weekly reminder that God's body and program are so much bigger than the lifestyle of an eighteen- to twenty-two-year-old. You need the rhythm of a Sunday morning service that teaches truth, leads you in worship, and allows you to connect with God's community. We have a God-given need planted within us for a reset after the end of a long week, to be once more grounded in God's presence, ready to face another Monday.

Above all, just pick a church. No church is perfect. No church will be everything you want. Find one with your top two or three traits and get plugged in.

How Do I Find Christian Friends?

Concern 41

"I get that I need Christian community to encourage me and help me grow, but where exactly am I supposed to find these people?"

I've said it before, and I'll say it again. If you are at all serious about your walk with Jesus, you need to regularly be reading God's Word, pressing into God's Spirit—that means praying, learning to hear His voice, asking God to help you obey Him—and spending time with God's people. You don't need to spend every waking moment with only Christian friends, but you do need to have some that you consistently interact with.

When I was in graduate school, I really struggled with this. My schedule was intense with full-time work and classes. I worked on campus as a hall director, and my team consisted of several other grad students who were in my master's program. Naturally, that group of people became my very best friends. I spent the vast majority of my time with them, whether at work or in class, not to mention the rest of my social calendar. They were my tribe. Not only did I get along with them and enjoy their company, but they understood my life and I, theirs. Since it required living on campus as a hall director and being on call over nights and weekends to respond to emergency situations, my job made for a strange lifestyle that few people understood. Few people except for, of course, the folks who also lived it. So that group became my family; our ties ran thicker than blood.

But none of them really shared my Christian faith. They all knew I was a believer, and we had some great talks about what I believed and what they believed, but no one was really at the same place I was. There were a handful of strong Christian girls in my master's program, but I wasn't that interested in pursuing friendships with them. I had my people; I didn't need a group of Christian friends—or so I thought. I went to church. I even sang in the church choir. (I liked to think I was the Mandy Moore of that Baptist church's choir.) I was the young, beloved soloist and loved my elderly friends—but I certainly wasn't sharing life with them. Still, I read my Bible and spent time in prayer. All in all, I thought I was doing just fine spiritually.

However, looking back, that time of life was one of the more spiritually dark seasons I've experienced. The terrifying part is I didn't even see it at the time. Most of us have gone through difficult spiritual seasons. We suffer from depression or grief, or God just feels far away. Yet we are aware of it, and we grasp for God as we struggle through it. But this was different. I didn't even realize how far from God I was. I was going through the motions, checking off the boxes, and thought I was just fine. But I wasn't growing. I wasn't being challenged or encouraged. I was stagnant. And the truth is that if you're not growing toward God, you're growing away from Him. While we may think we can remain stationary, there is no such thing. We are always in motion one way or another. And so I grew further and further away from God, without any awareness.

Not only did that season pervade the two years of my master's program, but I continued the pattern even after I graduated. I've mentioned before that the way you live your life in college will usually create habits that continue throughout the rest of your twenties and into adulthood. While I may not have begun to create this new pattern until graduate school, it became a formed habit just the same. I learned to exist without a Christian community, blind to my desperate need for it. I honestly don't know if I would have ever woken up from my slumbering faith, slowly moving away from God without any awareness of my direction. Yet, by the grace of God, a friend reached out and asked if I wanted to be in a Bible study led by her parents, with several other young professionals. While my closest inner circle at the time was still made up of work friends, most of whom did not share my Christian beliefs, that Bible study became my lifeline. It reinvigorated my soul. Suddenly, I was yearning to study the Bible again, grateful to be sharing prayer requests and grappling with deep issues of faith with like-minded people. We would send emails almost daily with a quick request for prayer, while the rest of the group would answer with their prayers of response typed out. We would remind one another to put on our spiritual armor (see Ephesians 6) when life was beating us down. God used that group of people to breathe new life into my spiritual journey.

And the same can happen for you. You cannot do this life of faith alone. So, of course, have friends who aren't believers. Share life with people who have differing beliefs from you, but, by all means, you must seek out a group of Christians who will hold you to a Christlike standard. A tribe who will pray for you, challenge you, and love you in a way only Christ-filled people can.

Finding other believers at college usually isn't that difficult, but it's up to you to seek them out, plug in, and commit to befriending them. So here's what you're going to do.

1. FIND A LIST OF ALL THE CHRISTIAN MINISTRIES AT YOUR COLLEGE.

There are probably several: Cru, InterVarsity, Fellowship of Christian Athletes, the Navigators, Young Life, Baptist Collegiate Ministry, Reformed University Fellowship, Delight Ministries. There are even Christian sororities. And that's just to name a few! Find out what your school has to offer and when those ministries meet.

Most of them will have a weekly large-group meeting and a small-group option.

2. CHECK THEM OUT.

Try to attend all the different large-group meetings. It may take you a few weeks to hit them all up, but see where you most easily connect, what feels most comfortable.

3. GET PLUGGED IN.

Just like my advice about church, you can't only sit back and consume a weekly large-group session. You have to get plugged in. Join a small group and faithfully attend. Get to know the other students in the group. Pursue them outside the weekly meeting. Christian community works only if you're sharing your life with those people. You have to be known, you have to be vulnerable, and they have to reciprocate.

4. REALIZE THAT IT'S OKAY IF THEY AREN'T YOUR BFFS.

A lot of people get flaky on small groups because they don't feel like the folks in their group are their BFFs. But God's body isn't filled with everyone who is like you. We get to learn from people who are different from us. Oftentimes, I find the most stretching relationships God puts in my life are people I wouldn't have necessarily picked out to be my friends. They have different perspectives and interests that reveal to me a different shade of our Savior. And that's a good thing! So don't flake on your group if you don't have an instant connection with the others who attend. Commit for the year. If by the end of the year you still aren't finding your place, then you can try a different small group once you go back to school in the fall. Remember, you get out of relationships what you put into them. If you don't pursue relationships with people in your group, you aren't going to connect. It's up to you to seek people out with intention.

I'm Terrified of Sharing My Faith
Concern 42

"I know Jesus has commanded us to share our
faith, but I am just so terrified. It seems like
such an awkward conversation. I have no idea
how to even bring it up, much less talk about
it in a way that doesn't offend or alienate my
non-Christian friends."

Call it what you want—evangelism, discipleship, sharing your testimony, or witnessing—if you grew up in the church, you likely
heard some pastor teach about Jesus' command to share your faith.
The unfortunate part is that all of those labels have complex layers,
meanings, and connotations that often leave us squirming in our
seats.

The hard pill to swallow is that if the gospel is really true, if
we are all sinners who deserve hell and Jesus is the only way—
not just for eternal life in heaven, but for abundant life here on
earth—we should have a deep desire to share our faith and see
our nonbelieving friends come to know Jesus. If hell is real—and
the Bible makes it pretty darn clear it is—it's not an ideal destination. If only out of motivation to save our friends and family
from eternal punishment, we should want to tell them the gospel.
But we don't. Why?

Growing up as a pastor's kid gave me a limitless faith in Jesus
and a strong conviction to tell others about Him. By age seven, I
could be found on the playground telling my friends about Jesus or

in class suggesting that *resurrection*, *tomb*, or *Savior* should be a bonus spelling word on our weekly quiz around Easter. I was fearless, and my love for Jesus abounding. I wanted all my friends to know about Him and how He loved them and died on the cross for them. But somewhere in my development, probably once my brain started understanding peer pressure, people-pleasing, and needing to fit in, I slowly stopped sharing the good news. I don't remember a specific moment or conversation that turned the tide. I just casually grew out of my childlike faith and conviction.

You may know Jesus' last words to His followers:

All authority in heaven and on earth has been given to me. Therefore go and make disciples of all nations, baptizing them in the name of the Father and of the Son and of the Holy Spirit, and teaching them to obey everything I have commanded you. And surely I am with you always, to the very end of the age. (Matthew 28:18–20 NIV)

Even though He was speaking only to His small group of eleven disciples, His words are just as prevalent for all of us today. Jesus is still saying to you and me, "Go and make disciples!" While most English translations say *go*, in the original language the New Testament was written in, the wording translates more exactly to, "As you are going, make disciples..." While those few words don't change the overall meaning, they do change how I imagine it. Too often, I think we hear "go and make disciples of all nations" and envision ourselves getting on a plane to Uganda, Mexico, or India. We travel to a destination in order to make disciples. But *as you are going* makes me envision my regular routine. As I go about my day at work, to social events, around my neighborhood, running errands, it's in those spaces that I am called to make disciples. Of course, it doesn't mean I can't fly to Guatemala or Slovenia to tell others about Jesus, but how often do we get to take those kinds of trips? Instead, we should consider as we are going, *Who has God put in my path to share the gospel with?*

I once heard *discipleship* defined as "following Jesus and inviting others along for the walk." I don't know about you, but that demystifies it for me.

Jesus told his disciples, "Follow Me, and I will make you fishers of men" (Matt. 4:19 NKJV). Following and fishing—they go hand in hand. It's also vital to notice that while we must obey the call to follow, Christ is the one who turns us into fishers. Of course, we have to step out in obedience to do that, but He is still the one who does the making. But, believe it or not, when you decided to follow Jesus, He turned you into a disciple maker. In fact, He created you to do just that!

Earlier, I mentioned that at minimum, we should be motivated to tell others about Jesus because of their eternal destination. But I believe that message is a large part of our nonchalance toward evangelism. We see the afterlife as just that—after life. It's second in priority in our hearts and minds to this life we're currently living. If knowing Jesus as your Savior is just about the afterlife, it's hard for there to be a sense of urgency. I mean, how often do you actually think about life after death? On the other hand, how often do you find yourself dreaming about, strategizing, and contemplating this life?

But what if knowing Jesus wasn't just about our eternal destination? What if it was vital to this life on earth? Well, it *is* vital! But do you believe that?

I believe that the first step in evangelism, discipleship, sharing your faith, or whatever you want to call it is a personal deep-rooted belief that following Jesus and living for Christ is a better story than living for the world.

Your life and mine should look different because we live for

Jesus. It should look better than lives without Jesus. And I don't mean in the works-based good-girl, churchy kind of way or in the "I have no problems, everything is perfect" kind of way. Of course, we will all have struggles and hardships like the rest of the world, but we should have more joy and more hope, and we should be able to extend more grace, living without burden and worry, because our anchor is in Jesus and not the world around us. If we were to truly live that way, our lives would be so appealing to those who don't!

We must be convinced that living for Christ is the best way to live. If you're already thinking, *You may have lost me there, Hanna*, that's where we need to start. Ask God to help you. Ask Him to give you a firm conviction that following Him, knowing Him, obeying Him, is the best possible story you can live. Ask Him to help you find the joy, peace, grace, and love that He's already planted inside you. Talk about this with your Christian friends or in your small group. How can you help one another live the abundant life that Jesus has already offered you? Christ didn't die on the cross just to save you from eternal damnation; He died on the cross so that He could have a relationship with you right now in this life. He rescued you so that you could be part of His kingdom here on earth. He adopted you so that you could step into a new identity as a daughter of the Most High King. You are His chosen child, and He is crazy about you! Shouldn't our lives look different if we fully believe that?

So that's step one. We have to first personally believe that knowing Jesus matters. Then the second part is *as you go*. Who has God already put in your life who is struggling, who needs a friend to care about them? Sharing your faith doesn't mean you need to pick a stranger and have a five-point gospel sermon prepared. It starts by being a good friend and naturally developing an open dialogue about things that matter, like your faith!

There was a book that came out when I was in college called

Questioning Evangelism. I, too, really struggled with the uncomfortable tension of how I was supposed to be obeying Jesus without being some evangelism freak. The main idea I took from that book was that instead of just launching into the gospel story or my own testimony, I should start by asking questions. Because the first option *is* awkward, right? I also imagined myself suddenly changing the subject from the latest *Friends* episode to, "So, Amanda...I really want to talk to you about something important and I've got my Bible right here...." What?! When in normal conversation do we ever do things like that? We don't come to our friends with a prerehearsed monologue in any other area of life. We just ask each other questions and start talking. And that is the best way to open the door to a spiritual conversation as well.

Ask your friends, "So what do you believe about God?" or "Does your family have any set of religious beliefs? What do you think about it all?" Ask your friends what they think about God, eternity, Jesus, whatever, and then *listen*. Just listen really closely and keep asking questions. Eventually they will ask you a question like, "Well, what do you think?" And then you get to share! You aren't pushing your beliefs on them; you're simply answering their question and having a mutual dialogue about faith and spirituality. Again, you don't have to give them a sermon or crack open your Bible. You answer the question they ask and see where it goes from there. It's a lifelong process.

Finally, remember that it's up to God to bring people to Him. You and I get to share our own stories with friends. We have the honor of telling others how Jesus has made all the difference in our lives, but that's where our job ends. God's Spirit really does all the work—He will even give you the words to share if you ask Him! Rely on His Spirit to show you who is ready for a spiritual conversation. Ask Him to give you the words. They won't come out perfectly, and that's okay. It's up to the Holy Spirit to influence your friends' hearts.

My prayer for you right now is that God gives you an overwhelming conviction that life with Him is the best life to have on this earth and then that He gives you His eyes to see a friend who is ready for a spiritual conversation. I'm also praying that you would have a natural opportunity to ask that friend about what they believe and see where it goes from there. It's not up to you to convince or convert them. God's Spirit does that! You just get to share what you know the Bible says and how that has transformed your life.

What Should I Do When It Feels Like God Has Gone Silent?

Concern 43

> "I have been praying for a specific situation for quite some time, and it just feels like God is not responding. What am I supposed to do? It feels like God has gone silent."

Anyone who has walked with Jesus for more than a minute has experienced this at one point or another. Well, maybe not just a minute, but you know what I mean. If you are consistently seeking God's presence and response, there will be times when it seems like He is so close you can almost touch Him. He responds so loudly and clearly you almost fall on your face. Yet other times, hello—where is He? He feels far away or silent. This is the Christian life. This is true faith. If we always felt God, if we always heard Him, how much faith would we need to have? I often wonder if the times He seems silent are the best seasons of growth for me. I have to be more patient, lean in closer, tune my ear, and have a deeper faith as I wait for Him to answer, or, even riskier, I have to make a decision based on wisdom alone.

Based on what the Bible tells us, sometimes there are real, concrete reasons why God isn't responding.

Isaiah 59:1–2 says:

> Surely the arm of the LORD is not too short to save, nor his ear too dull to hear. But your iniquities have separated you

from your God; your sins have hidden his face from you, so that he will not hear. (NIV)

James 4:1–3 says:

What causes fights and quarrels among you? Don't they come from your desires that battle within you? You desire but do not have, so you kill. You covet but you cannot get what you want, so you quarrel and fight. You do not have because you do not ask God. When you ask, you do not receive, because you ask with wrong motives, that you may spend what you get on your pleasures. (NIV)

While those may be hard verses to swallow, they make it pretty clear that God is not interested in answering our prayers when we are living in disobedience or when we ask with wrong motives. I have personally been at fault in both these ways before. It's not pretty, but it's always a fair question to ask yourself when faced with unanswered prayer.

There is another interesting excerpt in the Old Testament that relates to this. There was a king named Hezekiah who had his own stories of answered prayers when his motives were right and the wrath of God when his motives were wrong, which you can read about in 2 Chronicles 32. Yet there is this tricky little verse toward the end of the brief account of his reign that says, "However, when ambassadors arrived from Babylon to ask about the remarkable events that had taken place in the land, God withdrew from Hezekiah in order to test him and to see what was really in his heart" (2 Chron. 32:31 NLT).

Just earlier in Hezekiah's story, there were three accounts of when Hezekiah prayed and God responded. Yet in a moment when other rulers, folks whom Hezekiah would have wanted to impress, showed up—and by the way, we know from earlier in the account that Hezekiah, like most kings, struggled with pride—God literally left Hezekiah in order to test him. In other words, God was waiting to see how Hezekiah would respond when he could no longer sense His presence. Would he give God the glory for the remarkable events that had occurred, or would he take credit himself in order to impress the visiting rulers?

Now, I don't think God literally leaves us, like He left Hezekiah. After Christ's resurrection and departure, we were given the Holy Spirit (see John 16), which marks a drastic difference between us and Hezekiah. You and I are sealed with God's Spirit (see Ephesians 4) and therefore are never "left" like Hezekiah. God is always with us, because the Holy Spirit always indwells us. Jesus promised to never leave us or forsake us. How can He do that? Through the presence of His Holy Spirit. So you are never, ever without God. However, I do think that many times when we are looking to God to give us a strong yes or no, He keeps His mouth shut. He's not distant. He's not gone. He's letting you decide. And perhaps He's testing you. He has given you wisdom, discernment, the Holy Spirit, and His Word. Are you able to make a decision based on those things even when it feels like He's far?

So if you check your heart and you know you're not living in blatant sin and your motives aren't wrong, you can rest easy that God is not stringing you along, hoping you'll read the stars to see a sign from Him. After all, that doesn't line up very well with His character, does it? But sometimes He goes silent to test us, and other times, I think He just lets us make our own decisions.

God created you with a brilliant brain and strong instincts and gave you the Holy Spirit to guide your moral compass. He created you to make decisions, to take risks and create things. I think many times He just wants you and me to do something, to pick something! As long as it's not a moral decision, there probably isn't a "right" or "wrong" way to go. There may be a "better" choice, but sometimes all options are good and we need to just decide what we want to do. Too often we overspiritualize the decision-making process.

I'll leave you with one other thought. In Psalm 89, the psalmist spends the first thirty-seven verses declaring, over and over and over, God's faithfulness, loving-kindness, and awesomeness. Then at verse 38, everything changes, and we see that this whole time the songwriter has felt like God has gone silent. Verse 46 literally says, "How long, O Lord? Will you hide yourself forever?" (esv). Yet still at the end of the psalm, he says, "Blessed be the Lord forever! Amen and Amen" (esv). Take a minute and read it for yourself, and you'll see there is no resolution in this psalm. The psalmist doesn't suddenly say, "Ah, there you are, Lord! Thank you for answering me. AMEN!" Nope. In the midst of feeling like God has left him, he chooses to say, "Blessed be the Lord forever! Amen and Amen." How is he able to genuinely do that? Well, he spent the first thirty-seven verses reminding himself of God's true character.

And the same is true for you. It may *feel* like God is silent or far away, but the truth is that He is near and that He hears you. He may not answer, but another songwriter tells us, in Psalm 116, that He always hears. When it feels like God is far, we have to remind ourselves of His true character. God is faithful to you. He loves you like crazy. He has promised to never leave you or forsake you. So even when it feels like God is silent, we can make decisions and then say, "Blessed be the Lord forever."

How Do I Rejoice with Those Who Are Rejoicing When I'm Hurting?

Concern 44

"I've been hoping for some specific career opportunities that haven't panned out. At the same time, I'm watching a friend with similar interests find a lot of success. Each time my friend shares a new achievement with me, it's like a dagger in my chest. I want to be happy for her—I am happy for her—but the sting of jealousy and hurt is greater."

"'Tis the season of engagements and weddings! It seems like there is a constant flow of 'save the date' postcards and 'will you be my bridesmaid?' asks. While I'm so glad for my friends, the sting and hurt of my own recent breakup is stronger. Each wedding invitation is a reminder that the man I thought I would marry rejected me and I am once again single."

I don't know what your circumstance is, but I have found life to be full of this kind of thing. Your friend got the internship, the on-campus job, the camp counselor position, the guy, the *whatever*, and you didn't. She has what she wants, and you are left lacking. She's thrilled, and you're heartbroken. It's, at the very least, challenging. And depending on how we respond, it can even be ugly.

Proverbs 14:30 tells us, "Envy rots the bones" (NIV) and James

3:16 says, "For where you have envy and selfish ambition, there you find disorder and every evil practice" (NIV). Let's just call a spade a spade. The root of the problem here is jealousy. We are unable to be happy for our friends because, deep down, we're not just hurt; we're jealous. Their success makes our failure worse, because we have fallen into the trap of comparison and jealousy. So here's what we need to do:

CONFESS THE JEALOUSY.

Jealousy is a crazy monster who grows larger and larger when we ignore him or try to hide him in our closet. However, when we bring him into the light, he's like a vampire who instantly decays! I'm not saying you should tell your rejoicing friend that you are jealous, but you need to confess your jealousy to God and then possibly to another trusted friend. Ask your friend to pray for you. Ask her to follow up with you every week or two and ask how you are doing. When we admit our jealousy to God and a friend who can keep us accountable, we diminish its hold on us. The jealousy probably won't disappear altogether, but by confessing it to another, you are immediately weakening its power over you. Hidden jealousy will rule over you. Confessed jealousy allows you to be master of it.

DON'T COMPARE YOUR BEGINNING TO SOMEONE ELSE'S MIDDLE.

Oftentimes when we see someone else experiencing something we want, whether it's a meaningful dating relationship or marriage, career achievements, or financial success, we are looking at the middle of their story. But we are only at the beginning of ours. You can't compare your beginning to someone else's middle. It's an unfair comparison that will lead to even more jealousy and false expectations.

ASK GOD TO GIVE YOU A GENUINE JOY FOR YOUR FRIEND, BUNDLED UP RIGHT NEXT TO YOUR OWN HURT AND DISAPPOINTMENT.

What a beautiful picture when we can fully admit our own sadness while fully embracing joy for our friend. And it is possible! Rejoicing with those who rejoice does not mean we have to pretend we are okay. Your Savior wants you to bring all of your feelings to the table. Feelings of hurt, sadness, and disappointment are all things He knows and intimately cares about. And, unlike jealousy, those feelings are not sinful. They are our broken, human response to the imperfect world we live in.

It's easy to rejoice with others when you, too, are in a state of rejoicing. But it rarely seems to go that way, does it? Yet if we confess our jealousy and quit the comparison game, I know that God desires to give us genuine joy for one another—especially in the midst of our own disappointment. And when we accomplish that, when we are able to live in the tension of joy and hurt, I think our rejoicing with one another is all the sweeter.

I Don't Know What I Believe Anymore
Concern 45

> "I was raised in the church, but now I'm reconsidering everything I was taught to believe. So many doubts and questions are arising: What if Christianity isn't the only way? What if the Bible is just a collection of stories written by men who essentially created their own religion? Who are we to say that Christianity is more right than any other world religion?"

First, I want to say that your questions are valid and you *should* reconsider everything you were raised to believe. I know that it may seem scary or wrong to say you need to reconsider what you've been taught, but if you don't, I'm not convinced you'll ever truly own it.

I gave my life to Jesus when I was four years old. And I meant it. In my four-year-old brain, I understood that I was a sinner in need of a Savior, and I believed that Jesus was that Savior. It wasn't until middle school that I experienced my first crisis of faith. In a short time frame, my family experienced the deaths of several close friends. I began to struggle with the concept of a good and loving Heavenly Father who would allow such things to happen. These were good people who loved God. Why were they suddenly taken away from their spouses, children, and loved ones? How did that line up with the God I had been taught to trust, who promised to work all things for our good? In my time of wrestling, I found myself surrounded more by friends who denied God's existence, or at least rebelled against Him, than peers who actually believed in Jesus. I found books on Mormonism, Buddhism, Islam, anything I could get my hands around, to investigate other sets of religions and beliefs.

That wrestle lasted about two years, and it was a pivotal season of my life. While I certainly made some mistakes along the way, it was vital that I took time to consider the truth of the Bible and how it related to not only my seemingly conflicting life experiences, but also other so-called truths that people around the world devote their lives to. I couldn't just accept the truth that had been handed to me as truth because my parents or the church said so; I needed to discover that it was truth all on my own.

A few years later, I experienced another crisis of faith. This time, I didn't respond in rebellion or disbelief. Instead, I pressed into the truth I knew God had for me in His Word, in His presence, and with His people. This crisis of faith wasn't like the first one, when my life experiences at the time had caused me to doubt. Rather, this time I was in a dark place, and I knew the only way out was by clinging to Jesus. Due to a number of issues with performance-based acceptance, the need for success and recognition, perfectionism, and more, I had fallen into a state of depression with an eating disorder on the side. I was miserable. But for more than a year, I pretended to be fine. I continued to maintain my everything-is-perfect exterior while I was dying on the inside.

Each morning before school, I would pull into my parallel parking spot and spend about twenty minutes working through a Bible study called *Experiencing God*. After I completed the day's assignment, I would spend another fifteen minutes praying and listening to music but, really, bawling my eyes out. Then I'd give myself about five minutes to get it together, allow my face to turn back from cherry red to its normal pale olive, and head into school, where I pretended like everything was okay. While it breaks my heart to think about the girl I was, so sad, so alone, I know now that it was a pivotal time. I learned that in times of sorrow and disappointment, I had somewhere to turn. I learned that if I allow God's truth to wash over me long enough, if I keep seeking His face and desiring His help, He will draw near and eventually will heal my broken heart. Of course, at some point, I had to reach out to other people who could help me heal from depression and my eating disorder, but it took God's work on my heart before I was even able to trust anyone else.

If it were not for those two different seasons of crisis, I wonder who I would be today. My faith would certainly not be as grounded or deep. Since high school, I have faced countless times of hardship, but thanks to the process of discovering God's truth on my own and learning to lean into Him during difficult times, I now know how to stand firm on God's promises—even when my circumstances seem overwhelming.

I don't know what has caused your own crisis of faith, but I do know that God is allowing you to experience it. So don't shy away! Press into the Bible. Really read it. Study the life of Jesus. Study the bigger story of the Bible. Make it your mission to understand who God has revealed Himself to be in His Word. Find solid Christian books that discuss the topics you are struggling with. Ask the questions you can't find answers to. Reach out to your pastor, campus ministry leader, or any trusted, wise believer you can have some hard conversations with. They would love nothing more than to help you wrestle through your doubts and questions. Just keep pressing in.

Satan would love for you to become so overwhelmed with your doubts and questions that you allow them to slowly lead you away from Jesus. That's exactly what happens when we don't press in and find an anchor of truth to secure ourselves to. But if you earnestly try to find God's answers, I promise He will reveal Himself to you and take you on a journey of incredible depths and heights.

Jeremiah 29:13 says, "You will seek Me and find *Me* when you search for Me with all your heart" (NASB). Deuteronomy 4:29 says, "But from there you will seek the LORD your God, and you will find *Him* if you search for Him with all your heart and all your soul" (NASB). And one of my favorites, Proverbs 8:17, says, "I love those who love me, and those who seek me diligently will find me" (NKJV). That is God's promise to you. If you seek Him, if you seek truth, you will find Him. So don't become stunted or frozen in your season of doubt. Keep seeking! He is near, and He can't wait to reveal Himself to you.

What's God's Will for My Life?
Concern 46

> "I believe God has created me for a purpose and has a great plan for my life, but how exactly do I know what it is? How do I know what decisions to make or if I'm actually within His will or not?"

In Chapter Nine, I'll tell you about my formula and reflection process to discern what God may have wired you to do as your career. However, many of us still struggle with the larger idea of *What's God's will for my life?* What is His will, not just in your career and calling, but in regard to where you should live, how you should spend your money, what church you should go to, whether you should get married, whom you should marry, which car you should buy, which job offer you should take, whether you should buy a dog, whether you should have kids, how many kids you should have . . . I could go on. While God gave us the Bible, He certainly didn't give us step-by-step directions on how we should live our individual lives. So beyond reading the Bible and praying, how are we supposed to know God's will for every decision we need to make in this life?

Years ago, I read a marvelous book by Kevin DeYoung called *Just Do Something: A Liberating Approach to Finding God's Will or How to Make a Decision Without Dreams, Visions, Fleeces, Impressions, Open Doors, Random Bible Verses, Casting Lots, Liver Shivers, Writing in the Sky, Etc.* Longest and funniest book title ever, but it had a huge impact on my understanding of deciphering God's will.

The way Reverend DeYoung puts it is like this: You can think of God's will as a two-sided coin. One side is God's will of *decree*. The other side is God's will of *desire*.

A decree is an official order. Think about a king ordering a decree. What he decrees to happen is what happens. Reverend DeYoung says, "What God wills, will happen, and what happens is according to God's will." This is where we see God's sovereignty. Nothing can screw up God's sovereign plan and will of decree. He is ultimately in charge, and everything will happen according to His plan.

Two quick verses to contemplate:

> Remember the former things, those of long ago; I am God, and there is no other; I am God, and there is none like me. I make known the end from the beginning, from ancient times, what is still to come. I say, "My purpose will stand, and I will do all that I please." (Isaiah 46:9–10 NIV)

His purpose, His plans—they stand. He will accomplish exactly what He wants.

> Your eyes saw my unformed body; all the days ordained for me were written in your book before one of them came to be. (Psalm 139:16 NIV)

God is sovereign even over each day of your life. Before you were born, He determined the number of days that you would spend on this earth. *Ordained* is another word for "decreed." He said it would be so, so it will be so.

God's will of decree is the big picture. Now, the other side of the coin, God's will of desire, is a little different. We could say that God's will of decree is "how things are." His will of desire is "how God wants things to be."

The Bible has dozens and dozens of verses about God's will of desire for our individual lives and the earth as a whole. This is the way He wants us to live, but He won't force us to, because He desires for us to choose His way, not to be forced to obey. So what's God's will of desire for you? Here are just a few verses. (The bolding is mine, for emphasis.)

Do not love the world or anything in the world. If anyone loves the world, love for the Father is not in them. For everything in the world—the lust of the flesh, the lust of the eyes, and the pride of life—comes not from the Father but from the world. The world and its desires pass away, but whoever does **the will of God** lives forever. (1 John 2:15–17 NIV)

It is **God's will** that you should be sanctified: that you should avoid sexual immorality; that each of you should learn to control your own body in a way that is holy and honorable. (1 Thessalonians 4:3–4 NIV)

Submit yourselves for the Lord's sake to every human authority: whether to the emperor, as the supreme authority, or to governors, who are sent by him to punish those who do wrong and to commend those who do right. For it is **God's will** that by doing good you should silence the ignorant talk of foolish people. (1 Peter 2:13–15 NIV)

Rejoice always, pray continually, give thanks in all circumstances; for this is **God's will** for you in Christ Jesus. (1 Thessalonians 5:16–18 NIV)

God's will of desire is for you to not love the world but, rather, to love Him. God's will of desire is for you to be sanctified and holy, which includes avoiding sexual immorality. God's will of desire is for you to submit to authority placed over you. And—my personal favorite—God's will of desire is for you to rejoice always, pray all the time, and be thankful no matter what!

While I'm not trying to minimize the value of seeking God's direction for our lives, we spend far too much time wondering what He wants us to do in specific circumstances and practically ignore the instructions He has clearly written out for us in the Bible.

How desperate are you to know God's will for your life? How serious are you about walking in obedience to His will? Before we get caught up in the *direction* questions of our lives, are we earnestly attempting to live by His *desire* for our lives, as clearly seen in His Word?

God's ultimate will of desire for your life is that you grow more Christlike. And while most of us spend far too much time wondering and worrying about God's will for things like *What college should I go to? What job should I take? What house should I buy? What person should I marry?* I believe God cares way more about the *how* than the *what*. How you live your life, how you make decisions, how you treat others, how you love and obey Him. When we focus our minds on the *how* first, the *what* seems to fall in line.

God cares a whole lot about the moral aspects of our lives. Yet we spend a lot more time worrying and praying about the nonmoral aspects. All the questions I've already listed—all of these fall into the nonmoral areas of life.

In Matthew 6, Jesus is teaching His disciples and a massive crowd of people. He's telling them to not worry about life—what they will eat or drink or what they will wear. Those are the most basic needs of life, right? And, goodness, do we worry about so much more than just that. But at the end of His "don't worry" message,

He tells us that the antidote is this: "Seek the Kingdom of God above all else, and live righteously, and he will give you everything you need" (Matt. 6:33 NLT).

I believe that is the same antidote we can apply when we are wondering what God's will of direction is when making a certain decision. Rarely does God tell us what to do before we make a decision. Far more often, He gives us opportunities to use the wisdom and discernment He has already provided to choose and take risks! Don't you think He delights in watching us make decisions and make something of our lives without giving us step-by-step instructions? Yet the key to making right decisions is straight from Jesus' sermon. If we seek God's kingdom—in other words, His will of decree and desire—if we try to live in obedience to Him, He will direct our paths. That doesn't mean He will tell us what to do; it means He will be with us as we take our next step.

I hope that gives you a sense of freedom as you continue to seek God's will for all the days of your life. He loves you; He's with you; He has given you His Word, His Spirit, and His people. Trust that, and trust that He will align your steps as long as you keep your eyes on Him.

CHAPTER NINE

When I Grow Up

College Girl Concerns 47–52

I feel so sad and lost. This is what being an
adult must feel like.

—Rory Gilmore, *Gilmore Girls*

Most people don't grow up. Most people age.
They find parking spaces, honor their credit
cards, get married, have children, and call that
maturity. What that is, is aging.

—Maya Angelou, *A Wealth of Wisdom:
Legendary African American Elders Speak*

While college is about fun, socializing, and getting an education,
it's also about professionalism. I am a firm believer that the college
experience is so much more than just a means to an end; it's a
process that propels you into adulthood. Adulting doesn't mean
you have it all figured out. Any grown-up who tells you they do is
straight-up lying! Adulting *does* mean that you are comfortable in
your own skin, that you take responsibility for your life, and that
you have some general direction of who God has made you to be
and how He might want to use you in this world.

I Want to Change My Major
Concern 47

"I went to register for classes and nearly had a mental breakdown. I don't want to take these classes or be a music major anymore. I'M FREAKING OUT."

That was me. It was the end of my sophomore year, and I was supposed to be registering for my junior-year fall-semester classes. I woke up at oh dark hundred, because that's what you do when registration is a madhouse at your school. For the record, registration is a bloodbath at every school, not just yours.

It was 6:45 a.m., and I was looking over the classes I'd planned to register for (once I'd refreshed the page ten thousand times and I could actually submit). I can't even remember what classes I was looking at that day. What I do remember is the overwhelming feeling of anxiety, fear, and panic. *I do not want to be a music major anymore! I do not want to register for those classes!*

The feeling was so powerful, so all-consuming, that I completely lost it. I called my mom in a hysterical crying fit. Poor woman. I had always been extremely levelheaded and rational, and rarely emotional. She probably thought my leg had been cut off. Again, keep in mind it was 6:45 a.m.

Registering for classes is stressful as is, but my greater panic was this: If not music, *then what?!* I had spent my entire life thinking I'd graduate with a music degree. I was registering for my junior year of classes. If I didn't register for music classes right then and there, what was I going to register for? *What was I going to do with my life?! How would I ever graduate on time? How is a nineteen-year-old supposed to know what she wants to do for the rest of her life?!*

Major freak-out.

If this is you, follow these **five steps**:

1. TAKE A DEEP BREATH.

In fact, take several slow, deep breaths. Try to calm yourself. The world is not ending. You will figure it out. It will be okay. I promise.

2. JUST REGISTER FOR SOMETHING.

If you can't figure out what to do, just register for fifteen credits of general education classes that you still need. I'm pretty sure I freaked out so hard that I didn't register for anything. Don't do that. You have months to change your schedule.

3. UNDERSTAND THAT YOU ARE NOT GOING TO SOLVE THIS IN ONE DAY.

I didn't register for classes and then I headed straight to my academic advisor's office and sat in the hallway for what felt like hours until he was available to see me. Didn't he understand it was a 911 advising situation?! Nope. After I finally sat down with him, he wasn't even helpful. I actually remember feeling more discouraged and confused after we met. For some reason, I had put the expectation on myself that I would know *that day* what classes I should register for, what my new major should be, and what I wanted to do for the rest of my life. *That's insanity.* Furthermore, except in very rare cases, your academic advisor is probably not going to be great at helping you process what other major is a better fit for you. My advisor was a music professor. That's all he knew. He had no

information to give me about other majors outside the music de-
partment. In fact, he spent the whole time trying to convince me to
switch to music education. That's not his fault; that's his job. The
hard truth is that you aren't going to solve the complexities of this
confusion right away. Give yourself a break. You need some time to
chew on it.

4. FOCUS ON WHAT'S IN FRONT OF YOU RIGHT NOW.

I know these questions seem like the most important issue in your
life right now, but you need to focus on finishing the semester
strong. My meltdown bled into every day of the rest of the semester. Not good. You need to prioritize going to class, getting your
work done, preparing for finals, and hanging out with friends. Just
do the next thing. Again, you will figure out what to major in and
what you want to do with your life, but you're not going to this second, and you can't put everything else on hold until you do.

5. FIND THE RIGHT PEOPLE TO MEET WITH.

Maybe your realization that you don't like your major isn't as 911 as
mine. Regardless, finding the best major for you takes time and is a
process. Even if you're going into your junior year, you have time to
figure this out. Maybe you can't take a whole year, but you have at
least a few weeks or months! Over the rest of the semester, find out
who would be a good resource for you at your school. Most schools
have an office to help undecided students who need major or career
guidance. It might be your career center, a student success center, or
the counseling center. If you don't know where to start, ask an RA.
They usually know the right school resources to point you toward.
The "right people" might also include your parents, your boss, your
small-group leader, or anyone you trust and who knows you well.

*　　*　　*

During my months of exploration, I read the course catalogue from cover to cover about a dozen times. Today, all universities have their course catalogue online, which basically lists every major and minor available at your school with a brief description of all of the classes. After narrowing in on a few majors, I set up appointments with advisors or professors in those fields. I spent time investigating, not just the courses that I would need to take, but what kind of careers naturally came from those majors. Ironically, I didn't end up choosing a major that had a strong career outcome. I chose a major that sounded really interesting to me. My best advice when talking with students who are undecided is to pick a major that will get you out of bed and to class on time. That may seem a little too simple, but I think if we choose classes that intrigue us enough to do that, we've got to be on the right track—even if that track doesn't have an obvious career landing.

Again, take a deep breath. Remind yourself that it doesn't have to be fixed today. You can go at least two semesters in college (and possibly even two full years) without a major and simply knock out your gen eds. Take time to explore other majors, classes, and career fields before committing to something else.

What Do I Want to Be When I Grow Up?
Concern 48

"I finally declared a major in communications, because it seemed generic enough to work for any job. But as I get closer to graduation, I realize I still have no idea what I want to do with my life. How am I supposed to figure out what I want to be when I grow up?"

Statistics today show that at least 50 percent of entering college students are undecided about their majors. And 50 to 70 percent of students change their major at least once, though most will change their major at least three times before they graduate.[1] Many recent college graduates will change jobs four times by the time they are thirty-two.[2] While I may be a bit older than you, I am still a walking example of those last two stats. I changed my major several times in my mind, though only twice on paper, and I am on my fourth job!

The idea that an eighteen-year-old, or even a twenty-two-year-old, should know what she wants to do with her life is absurd. Yet in these four years, you have to choose a major, internships, and a first full-time job—all of which seem to have a huge impact on how you will spend the rest of your life.

From eighteen to twenty-two, I was fairly tormented with those questions. My entire life, I had set my eyes on a career in music. Everything I did in high school was motivated by the goal to go to the best music school possible, so that I could have a career as an artist. After two long and tumultuous years as a music major—struggling with the fact that I was no longer the best in the room, nor was I willing to work as hard as others—I knew it was time to let go of the music career dream.

But it felt as if the wind had been knocked out of me. I had spent the last two decades of my life fixated on a career that I was no longer motivated to seek. Twenty years of experience, practice, performances, résumé building...all for nothing.

The following two years of college were a whirlwind. Every month, I had a new plan for my life, a new major to declare, a new graduate studies program to consider. Now that I no longer had tunnel vision for music, the world was wide-open with limitless possibilities. I was overwhelmed with career options.

Then one day, during a quick trip to Chicago to visit my family, I found myself sitting in a student chapel service at Moody Bible Institute. It was the middle of my senior year, and I was still desperately searching for my career and calling. Howard Hendricks, longtime professor at Dallas Theological Seminary, took the stage and said in his confident and punctuated voice, "Today I am going to give you the formula of how to figure out your career and calling." He probably didn't say those exact words, but that's what I heard, and I was on the edge of my seat.

Dr. Hendricks went on to give a thirty-minute message that truly changed the trajectory of my life. For me, his entire message could be boiled down to one simple sentence: When deciding what to do with your life, consider the intersection of your strengths and your experiences.

What strengths and abilities has God prewired into you? What experiences has God already placed in your life?

Dr. Hendricks convinced me that if I pondered those two questions and considered the intersection where they met, I would find my answer.

And you know what? It worked! I realized I wanted to be a college administrator, to work with college students and help them along their journey as they figure out who they are, what they believe, and what they want to do with their life. From that moment forward, I didn't question or waver—I knew what my career and calling were, and I never looked back. Well, at least for a while.

Yet something happened about ten years into my career. Though my passion and love for college students hadn't changed, some of my life priorities had shifted, and for several reasons I found myself leaving my beloved higher-education career. While I didn't doubt my decision to change jobs, I wasn't sure how it fit with this "strengths-and-experiences intersection" theory. Had I somehow missed the mark or, should I say, my intersection?

The first house I bought in Nashville was off an intersection called Nippers Corner. Yes, I think it's a horrible name too, but even beyond the name, Nippers Corner confounds me. With four sides of the intersection, Nippers Corner boasts three grocery stores, three nail salons, three liquor stores, two State Farm agents, three chicken fast-food joints, three sub shops, two pizza places, several other fast-food options, and a wide variety of other stores and services.

I can't be entirely sure what Dr. Hendricks was imagining when he passed on his intersection theory to all of the college students in attendance, but I am fairly certain he wasn't imagining it the way I originally did—which was a tiny dot within the very center, where my experiences and strengths crossed paths. I took the intersection picture as the formula to finding *the* career or *the* calling God created me for.

But if we consider an actual intersection—like Nippers Corner—we realize there are so many options, so many things to explore. We can take the analogy even further with the many duplicates (grocery stores, chicken joints, etc.). My intersection of strengths and experiences probably has several "duplicates"—jobs and career fields that have a lot of similarities. But the intersection is also filled with lots of diversity and choice as well.

There are so many more choices, so much more freedom than I had ever imagined, at the intersection of my strengths and experiences.

So when choosing a major, an internship, a career field, your first job, or anything, consider your intersection. I believe this applies for the rest of our lives. No matter what age or season of life you are in, remember: God has given you a unique set of skills, strengths, and abilities, and He has also given you a perfectly unique story filled with a set of experiences that no one else has had. And where those things meet is perhaps the best place to find your direction, purpose, career, and calling. But know there are so many options at your God-designed intersection.

You may be thinking, *Well, that's all fine and good, Hanna, but how am I even supposed to figure out what's at my intersection?*

That is one of my favorite questions of all time. And this is what I want you to do:

1. REFLECT.

Go to a coffee shop or another favorite spot where you can reflect and process. Set aside at least an hour to do this. Remove distractions. No phone, no friend—just you and a cozy spot.

2. IDENTIFY.

Write down every job or experience you've ever had (leadership positions, sports, music, activities, mission trips, etc.). Go back as far in life as makes sense. If you have significant memories only from high school on, that's just fine. If you volunteered in the church nursery while in middle school and loved every second of it, that's important. If you won a young author competition in elementary school and it was one of the highlights of your life, write it down. Any job or experience you've had that stands out is worth processing.

3. DRILL DOWN.

Next to each role, write down what it was about those jobs/roles that you really enjoyed or that made you feel really good about yourself. Really push yourself to thoroughly reflect. Did you love problem solving? Helping people? Spending time with young children? Building or creating new things? Being behind the scenes? Being front and center? The overall environment or team you worked with? If you had jobs where you hated every aspect, write those down too.

4. LOOK FOR THEMES.

Are there three or four themes that keep popping up? If you don't see them at first, keep looking. When you find them, circle them. Perhaps you'll find several things that relate and can be relabeled under one theme.

5. BRAINSTORM.

Take some time to brainstorm by yourself. What types of jobs or industries can you identify that touch those three or four themes you've noticed? These themes may be skills you utilized, tasks you had, or certain aspects of the environment you thrived in. If you really struggle identifying related jobs or industries, consider taking your themes to a career counselor at your college. Your career center would love to help you brainstorm career fields, especially with the reflection work you've already completed in advance!

6. PROCESS IT.

After you've spent time brainstorming, I want you to go process it with a few different folks. I would recommend your parents, a trusted faculty or staff member (or a mentor of some sort), and a couple of your best friends. Ask them what they picture you doing, or what other strengths they see in you that you may not have identified.

God has uniquely wired you and given you special gifts. He has also already given you tons of experiences that have highlighted and strengthened those unique talents. Consider these two things (your strengths and your experiences) and see how you can pick a career based on them. But above all, just pick something. Anything. Your career isn't the be-all and end-all. Don't try to find all of life's fulfillment in your job. Pick something that you think you'll enjoy and that you are decently good at. If you try it out for a few years and decide you want to do something different, then you can do something different!

Press on, sister. Finish that degree and turn your sights toward a job that fits your talents, interests, and experiences. Your goal should be to pick a job that you can do for at least a year, preferably two. Then you get to reassess. All these "huge" life decisions aren't really as dramatic as we make them out to be. One day at a time. One decision at a time. You've got this.

Facing Rejection (from a Job, an Internship, or a Leadership Position)
Concern 49

> "I really wanted to be an orientation leader for the summer, but I just found out I didn't get the job. I am so bummed and can't help but feel like I drew the short stick and am going to miss out on a really awesome experience. To top it off, two of my best friends did get the job."

Whether we're athletes, musicians, actors, or mathletes, at some point in our childhood, we began the process of "trying out" for teams or auditioning for certain roles or opportunities.

Eventually, we all experience rejection. Maybe you didn't make the varsity squad or get the role you wanted in your high school play. Perhaps you didn't get accepted into your first-choice college. Or you didn't get the internship you wanted or the on-campus job you had your eye on.

The longer we live life, the more rejection we will face. Isn't that cheery?

BUT WHAT IF REJECTION DOESN'T HAVE TO BE TAKEN PERSONALLY?

When I was in high school, a musical theater director of mine introduced me to his personal theory, which I call "the bagel theory." It goes like this: All of us musical theater kids, we were bagels. My friend Chloe was a chocolate-chip bagel; my friend Anna was a blueberry bagel; I was an asiago cheese bagel. You get the idea. We were all delicious bagels, but we were each a different kind of bagel.

When auditioning for a new show, Chloe, Anna, and I could all be up for the same part. We would all be uniquely great for the role, but at the end of the day, the casting director was looking for a certain type of bagel. Chloe may have gotten the gig because they were looking for a chocolate-chip bagel. It didn't mean that Anna and I weren't amazing bagels. We just weren't the kind of bagel they were looking for.

Suddenly, getting rejected for a part wasn't a judgment of our talents or abilities; it was just a reflection of someone else's preferences. While I don't audition for musical theater roles anymore, the bagel theory has truly shaped how I look at every interview or opportunity I seek.

Now, buckle up, because here's where I like to combine the bagel theory with the sovereignty of God. My job is to work hard, be prepared, and show up for the opportunity. I just need to be the best darn asiago cheese bagel God has created me to be. Then if it is the right job, internship, college, or other opportunity for me, God will take care of the rest.

So now when I am rejected, not only is it not a reflection of my value, but I can trust in God's sovereignty. That opportunity just wasn't His best for me!

"But you can always find someone who is better, stronger, smarter, faster, or prettier than you," you might say.

Totally. I'm not trying to ignore the fact that every person is given a unique set of skills and abilities. But that's exactly my point: God has given you a distinctive set of skills, talents, and abilities. He is going to open the doors to opportunities that He has planned out for you. He's also going to close doors that you and I think are perfect for us, because He has another path in mind.

The longer I live, the more and more thankful I am when God closes a door. I only want to be exactly where He wants me to be. Rejection is no longer a reflection of my worth. It's a reflection of God's sovereign hand over my life.

So if you're currently licking your own "rejected" wounds, hear me out. This rejection is not a reflection of your personal worth— even if it's a romantic rejection. You are uniquely made—perfectly made, in fact—by your Heavenly Father, and He has great plans in store for you. This particular situation happens to not be one of them. Trust in Him and trust that He made you to be a great bagel!

> For we are His workmanship, created in Christ Jesus for good works, which God prepared beforehand so that we would walk in them. (Ephesians 2:10 NASB)

I'm So Busy I Don't Know if I'll Survive

Concern 50

> "I am juggling a hundred and one things over here and am so overwhelmed. Between classes, my internship, a campus job, two leadership positions, and student organization meetings, I don't know when I'm supposed to have a social life or even get it all done!"

I was sitting at the kitchen table, practically crying to my mom. My schedule had gotten out of control. I was so busy and tired, and I just needed to vent to someone about it. "No one's impressed," she said. Like a bullet to the heart. It may seem harsh, but that's my momma. Speaks truth like it is. No sugarcoating. She has the discernment to know when you can take it straight and when you might need it wrapped in a hug. "Honey, no one is impressed by how busy you are."

We've all been insanely busy. The seasons when your schedule is out of control and you're barely surviving: not enough sleep, not enough quality time with the important people in your life, not enough quality time with God, not enough rest (which is different from sleep, y'all!), and definitely not enough time for an actual personal life. When you and I get that busy, everyone gets the short end of the stick. Including ourselves.

At some point along the way, you and I believed our culture's lie that busyness is next to godliness. If you aren't busy, you're not important. You're not hustling enough. You're not contributing enough. You're not valuable enough. You're not enough.

Being busy is king. We think our crazy schedules should be admired. That people should recognize how busy we are and realize how important and impressive we are.

But what does being too busy really mean? It means you're a slave to your schedule. It means you aren't prioritizing well. It means you aren't letting go of things that need to be let go. It probably means you aren't spending quality time with the people you love. It definitely means you aren't taking care of yourself. And like my momma would say, that's not really impressive.

So how do you and I get out of the busy trap?

1. Stop glorifying your busy schedule. Remind yourself that no one is impressed. Being busy doesn't mean you're Superwoman. It means you're overworked and your schedule is out of control.
2. Say no. That two-letter word can be so hard to say, but if you're too busy, say it. Say no to everything—and I do mean everything—until you start feeling balanced again.
3. Look at how you've been spending your time and see what top priorities you've been neglecting. For me the top priorities that always go first are time with my face in the Bible, quality time with my husband, set time to actually rest and relax, and time for working out. I can't expect to feel like I'm doing more than barely surviving if I'm not doing these things. Yet they're always the first things to go when my schedule gets busy.

A quick word about resting: If you look up the verb *rest* in the Merriam-Webster dictionary online, you'll find a list of definitions. The first few are what you'd expect, but two of my favorites are: "to stop using (something) so that it can become strong again," and "to be free from anxiety or disturbance."

True resting should make us strong again. True resting should free us from anxiety. I came to this conclusion during a time in my life when "resting" usually took the form of lying on the couch and binge-watching Netflix. Now, I'm not going to knock binge-watching. There is a place and a time for it, but it isn't something that helps me feel strong or free from anxiety. Am I right? Things that do make me feel strong and help free me from anxiety: opening the windows in our house, listening to music, dancing in the kitchen with my husband, prepping and cooking something fun or elaborate, going on an early morning hike in the fall, spending time curled up with a book, carving out intentional quiet/alone time... My list could go on.

While these things bring me true rest, some take planning and effort. Yet that is real rest. Don't fool yourself into thinking that watching TV or scrolling through social media is rest. It's not. Find out what makes you feel strong and free from anxiety. Make a list and refer back to it when you know you need to make time for rest in your schedule.

So let's stop the insanity. Stop the busyness. As my momma would say, "No one's impressed anyway." And if we were sitting together at my kitchen table, I'd reach over to give you a big hug, just like my momma.

Come to me, all you who are weary and burdened, and I will give you rest. Take my yoke upon you and learn from me, for I am gentle and humble in heart, and you will find rest for your souls. For my yoke is easy and my burden is light. (Matthew 11:28–30 NIV)

How Do I Find Balance?

Concern 51

"How do I balance a social life, good grades, and enough sleep in college?"

Welcome to the rest of your life: finding balance. I would be lying to you if I said I mastered this in college, or even that I am a master of balance now. A few years ago, I came across an article titled "Nine Things Everyone Should Be Able to Do by Age 30," and number nine was to establish a work-life balance. A quote from the article reads, "Some experts have argued that the key is less about work-life *balance* than work-life *purpose*, or prioritizing what's important to you and fitting it into a composite of who you are, and what you do with your time."[3] I couldn't agree more.

I'm a huge fan of *Bittersweet* by Shauna Niequist. It is one of the most formative books I read in my twenties. Every chapter has a nugget of truth I've clung to, but one chapter in particular really affected me. Shauna writes, "I love the illusion of being able to do it all, and I'm fascinated with people who seem to do that, who have challenging careers and beautiful homes and vibrant minds and well-tended abs. . . . One of my core fears is that someone would think I can't handle as much as the next person."

I don't know about you, but that really resonates with me. I want to do it all and be seen like I can do it all. I want people to think I'm Superwoman. And that's probably my biggest challenge in finding balance. I say that I want balance, but deep down, I'm not willing to admit I can't do it all, which would create the balance I desperately need.

Shauna goes on to say, "It's not hard to decide what you want your life to be about. What's hard . . . is figuring out what you're willing to give up in order to do the things you really care about."

That kind of makes me break out in hives. How about you? Yet with all that in mind, here are a few things for you to think through in order to help you find balance.

1. WHAT ARE YOUR WEEKLY PRIORITIES?

Every college girl needs help balancing her social life, grades, and sleep, but are there other values or priorities you have? What are the things you need to accomplish or experience every week for you to be doing "what you want your life to be about"?

2. WHAT CAN YOU CUT?

I find this is much harder for college students to answer than college graduates. There are a lot of things you have to do (go to class, read your books, write papers, intern), which you simply can't cut. I get that. But surely there is something you can cut that isn't contributing to your top priorities.

3. WHAT IS THE IMMEDIATE PRIORITY?

When making decisions in the moment—like whether to stay in and write a paper or go to a party with your friends—ask yourself, *What is the immediate priority?* If the paper is due tomorrow, that's the immediate priority. If it's not due for a few days but you know that in order to get a good grade you need to start working on it now, the question becomes *Do I care more about an A or about hanging out with my friends tonight?* Your parents will hate me for saying this, but choosing the A doesn't have to be your decision. It usually was for me, but I have plenty of friends who would choose to relax and spend time with friends and take the B. Looking back, I wonder if I should have cut myself some more slack.

4. HOW ARE YOU SPENDING YOUR TIME?

We often waste precious hours in the day without realizing it. My favorite time-management activity, which helps you track your week in thirty-minute increments, came from an RA training class. I did it every year, even in grad school. You can find a printable version of the weekly schedule on the resource page of my website (hannaseymour.com). Don't try to alter your schedule because you're tracking your time. Just live life like you normally would and record it. Then after a week, go back and see where you wasted time or if there were things you can cut out in the future. Most times, this exercise shows we waste too much time on social media, YouTube, or TV. It may also show that you spent hours dealing with and discussing girl drama. Or maybe you just piddle around your room too much on the weekends. Whatever your time-wasting vice is, we often don't realize how many hours we waste until we do an exercise like tracking our time for a week. Try it and see what you learn!

5. ARE YOU BUILDING IN TIME TO RELAX?

It's okay to watch TV or read a non-school-related book. Or play your guitar. Or take a nap. Don't get so overly obsessed with time management and balance that you don't allow yourself to relax, blow off steam, or just hang out. That stuff is important too. It keeps us sane.

Graduation Is Around the Corner, and I'm Freaking Out

Concern 52

"Graduation is forty-seven days away. Don't get me wrong—I'll be thrilled to be done with classes, but then reality will be pounding at my door. I have no job, no prospects, and no idea where I'm going to live. Basically, I have no plan and am totally freaking out."

Graduation is right around the corner, and you have no clue what the future holds. Just imagining the stress and anxiety you're facing gives me that horrible knot in the pit of my stomach. Sister, I feel your pain! But before we start hyperventilating over this, let's take it one step at a time.

1. TAKE FIVE BIG, SLOW, DEEP BREATHS.

Inhale for ten seconds. Exhale for ten seconds. No, I'm not kidding. Do it. If you are feeling physical angst due to your unknown future, I need you to calm yourself down. Breathing exercises are a great way to do that. I went to a counselor during graduate school when I was experiencing some unusual stress-related issues, and breathing exercises became a big part of my coping strategy. Focusing on your breathing does something for your mind and body that I just can't explain. I would also recommend repeating to yourself over and over, *It's going to be okay. It's going to be okay.* Because it is! It is going to be okay. I promise.

2. PULL OUT A PIECE OF PAPER AND A PEN, AND WRITE DOWN YOUR *REALISTIC* WORST-CASE SCENARIO.

A nonrealistic worst-case scenario ends with you living in a cardboard box down by the river. Honestly, y'all. That's not going to happen. Don't let your imagination get the best of you. A realistic worst-case scenario might be moving back in with your parents or maybe taking a job waiting tables for a season. Seriously, do this exercise. I want you to put it down in writing and really look at it.

My realistic worst-case scenario would have been: I'd have to stay in Harrisonburg, Virginia, find a cheap place to live—probably in a house with a bunch of younger girls—and get a job at Outback Steakhouse. I would need to make enough to pay my rent, car insurance, and phone bill, and buy food. And I'd need a game plan to continue my job search.

Why am I so intent on you charting out your worst-case scenario? Because I want you to see that it's not the worst thing in the world. Sure, it's not your dream, but anyone over the age of thirty would read my worst-case scenario and think, *So?* The world is not ending here. You are just entering one of the harder transition phases of life—from full-time student to full-time adult!

The other reason I want you to write out your worst-case scenario is because I want you to be prepared for it. The reality is some of you **will** live your worst-case scenario for three months, six months, or even a year. It's just the reality of the situation. But as long as you don't lose your focus in continuing your job search, it is totally okay to make ends meet by waiting tables for a season. Get a job that helps pay the bills and shows you have a good work ethic, and keep up your dream job search!

3. WRITE DOWN YOUR GAME PLAN FOR FINDING THE JOB YOU WANT.

Create steps, goals, and due dates. If you don't know where to begin, visit your college's career center. A great place to start is picking a few target companies—where you'd love to work—and reaching out to an alum or another connection there to have an informational interview. An informational interview isn't a time when someone interviews you for a specific job opening. It's a time when you meet someone over coffee and ask them about their career story. What was their college transition to full-time employment like? How long have they been working in their current job? What do they love about it? What do they find most challenging? What advice would they give someone who is interested in their career field? Show them your résumé, and ask them what skills or experiences you need to garner in order to be a strong candidate for their company or field? It's a casual conversation, where you come prepared with questions to learn more about that person's job, their company, and any advice they can give you. You don't ask them to hire you. You don't ask for any favors. In fact, if you can swing it, you buy their cup of coffee. Seriously, do this. This is how you make connections and build friendships in the working world.

Speaking of connections, don't be afraid to use the connections you have—even if the connection is Mom or Dad. I see too many students shy away from using their parents' contacts. I used to be that way too. WHY?! God gave you your parents. Maybe He also gave you their connections for a reason!

4. THROUGHOUT THE NEXT SEVERAL WEEKS, ASK OLDER PEOPLE (ANYONE MORE THAN TWO YEARS OLDER THAN YOU) ABOUT THEIR JOURNEY FROM COLLEGE GRADUATION TO THEIR FIRST JOB.

Learn from others. You will find advice and encouragement in all kinds of places if you just look for it. No one will have a story just like yours, but everyone's story has value and something to offer. Choose to let others' stories encourage you—*not* add additional stress and anxiety. Walk away from each conversation and identify one or two lessons you can take from each story.

5. SERIOUSLY, CHILL OUT.

You are entering a season of waiting. It won't be terribly long, but this is a typical life transition that requires waiting. You'll have many more seasons of waiting throughout life, so think of this as good practice. The job offer will come; it's just a matter of timing. Be patient. Be diligent. Be prepared. Trust in our God, who has brought you this far! Hasn't He been faithful?

Two of my favorite verses to cling to during times like this are:

> In their hearts humans plan their course, but the LORD establishes their steps. (Proverbs 16:9 NIV)

You can plan your course all you want, but in the end, God determines where you actually go. It's great to dream and plan, but we have to hold those plans loosely, consult God in prayer, and trust that He will lead your steps exactly where He wants you to go. While that may be hard for some of us control freaks to swallow, I find such freedom in that. I am so thankful that at the end of the day God determines my steps. I have made some great plans for my life, but you know what? I really just want to be where He wants me to be, because I believe that His plan is ultimately better than mine. The older I get, the more He proves that to be true. He knows just where to lead you; you just have to keep your eyes and ears open, and follow!

> Cast all your anxiety on him because he cares for you. (1 Peter 5:7 NIV)

This is one of those verses I would meditate on during my breathing exercises. I needed to remind myself over and over that the best place for my anxiety was at the feet of Jesus. Why? Because He cares about me. He cares about me and my anxieties, and He is much better equipped to handle my worries than I am. God loves you. He cares about you, and He has great plans for you. Trust Him, and hand over your anxiety and the need to control everything. He's got this!

Last-Semester-of-College Bucket List

1. Do something legendary. Seriously. Plan a night for you and your closest friends that you will never forget. Do something you've always wanted to do. Be creative. Ask friends for input. Have your goal be to create an incredible out-of-the-box memory with people you really enjoy.

2. Write at least three handwritten thank-you notes to faculty or staff who have really supported, encouraged, challenged, or grown you. Those people almost never get thanked. If you had an advisor who saved your tush and waved a magic wand to help you graduate, buy them a present. Even if it's a ten-dollar gift card to the local coffee shop. A small gift will mean way more to them than you would imagine. Now is a great time to show gratitude and appreciation of others.

3. Go on a photo shoot excursion around campus. Grab your phone (or buy a disposable camera) and take pictures of all your favorite spots and sights. Take a picture of that tree you always lean against on the quad. Your freshman residence hall. The scenic view of the fountain.

It may sound stupid, but trust me—you'll be so glad you have them a few years from now. Even better, add this to your "legendary night with friends" and do a photo shoot with them all over campus. Then buy a photo album and print off as many college pictures as you can (or have a book printed through one of the online photo sites that does it all for you). I know that seems so outdated now, but just trust me and do it. You'll thank me later.

4. Eat in the cafeteria one more time. Some of you still do this all the time and some of you haven't stepped foot in there since the end of your sophomore year. Go be nostalgic. Grab a meal with some friends in the cafeteria and reminisce about what you were like as a little freshman. Talk about how you've changed, your best memories on campus, what you would do differently, and other fun reflections.

5. View every day as a chance to make a memory. Use this time as an excuse to be warm and fuzzy. Tell your besties how much they mean to you and how grateful you are for your time with them. Take risks. Be random. Don't let the stress of the end of the year overwhelm you. Finish your papers and projects, take your exams, but don't sweat it. Let these last few weeks be about people and enjoying the final part of this life chapter.

PART THREE

Moving On

CHAPTER TEN

What's Next?

Since your junior year of high school, well-meaning friends, family, and others have asked you a myriad of questions: Where are you applying for college? What's your reach school? Your safety school? How are your test scores? What will you be majoring in? Do you know what you're going to do with that degree? Do you have any internships lined up? Where will you be living? Anyone special in your life?

You may have noticed the onslaught of these questions as you neared high school graduation, but they likely haven't gone away, even as you round the corner toward college graduation. No matter what form the questions take, here's what everyone is really asking you: *What's next?*

What's next? is a loaded question. It's a stress-inducing question. It often makes my pits sweat and my heart race. *What's next?* has kept me up at night. *What's next?* has sent me to counseling. I realize I'm sounding like a basket case, but I swear I am a fairly grounded person. But *What's next?* can be a heavy question to deal with when you really have no clue how to answer it.

I have good news and bad news for you. I'll start with the bad, because I always prefer to end on a positive note. I've never understood folks who want the good first before learning the bad. If that's you, I suppose you could just read the rest of the chapter backward, but maybe you'll just stick with me and trust me to start with the bad.

*   *   *

The bad news is this: The **What's next?** question is never really going away. You may think that once you land your first job out of college the questions will stop, but instead they will continue coming in waves for the rest of your life.

What's your five-year plan? When do you hope to get a promotion? What's job number two? Think you'll go to graduate school? Are you dating anyone? Is it serious? When will you get engaged? What's the date for the wedding? Are you planning on buying a house? Are you going to have kids? How many kids? Will you stay home full-time or continue to have a career? Do you think you will stay in this city forever? Where else would you go?

Once I finally figured out what I wanted to do postcollege, I had a pretty solid plan. I would graduate (obviously), move in with my parents for the summer, and then head to South Carolina for graduate school. I was going to work as a residence director, which would take care of my grad school tuition and housing and give me a little stipend for living expenses. Then I'd graduate two years later and find a full-time job at another university. I would narrow my search to Atlanta, the North Carolina Triangle, and Washington, DC. All in all, I stayed the course and did just that.

I was happy. I'm a planner by nature, and it made me feel good to have accomplished what I set out to do. Yet only a year into my wonderful full-time DC job, it hit me: I had no idea what was next. Sure, I knew I wanted to move up or out after being in that job for two or three years, and I could have pieced together some idea of where that would be and what that would look like, but I really didn't know how it would unfold. I didn't know if I wanted to keep living in DC or try a new city. I was really clueless when it came to the whole fall-in-love-and-get-married area. I hadn't dated anyone seriously since college, and there was no guy in the foreseeable future. How was I ever going to meet someone? Would I actually get married someday? Would I ever have kids? Did I even want to be a mom?

Up until about the age of twenty-two, your life has been completely mapped out for you. Sure, there have been unknown bends and turns along the way, but generally you knew where you were headed. You went from elementary school to middle school to high school. You labored all of high school with the number one goal of graduating just so you could advance to college. You went to college with the goal of graduating so you could get a decent job, and maybe even the hope that you'd meet your future husband. Perhaps, like me, you even knew you'd go straight into graduate school. But at some point, whether at twenty-two or twenty-five, or even much later if you go the medical school route, your life stops being predetermined. There is no obvious next step.

And that's what makes this next chapter of life combined with the weighted *What's next?* question so daunting. The options are endless and, ultimately, very much out of your control.

That's the bad news. The *What's next?* never goes away, and you never really have the answers. And the question doesn't just come from other people; it will come from within yourself. Every few years, you'll find your own head and heart wrestling with *What's next?* What do you want out of life? What can you actually control? How do God's plan and sovereignty factor into the equation?

The only solution I've found to this bad news is acceptance and trust. You have to accept the fact that the *What's next?* never goes away. I have a yoga DVD by Jillian Michaels (she can be so mean, but I just love her), and at one point she yells, "GET COMFORT-ABLE WITH BEING UNCOMFORTABLE." That's actually a pretty good motto for life. Get comfortable with not knowing what's next. Get comfortable with the fact that you are ultimately not in control.

And then trust. Trust that God *is* in control. Trust that *He* knows what's next. Trust that if you keep your eyes on Him, He will lead you to the next thing and the next thing. Trust that He has a good plan for your life and is always working things out for your good. Trust that His timing and provision are better than what you could dream up. Trust Him.

Now on to the good news. And this is easily within the top five best pieces of news I have ever been told. The incredible, life-giving news is that the answer to *What's next?* doesn't define you. It doesn't determine your worth or value. It doesn't define your identity. It doesn't decide if you are a success or a failure. It doesn't determine if God loves you. It doesn't even determine if He is pleased with you.

Maybe that news isn't so earth-shattering to you, but it flies in the face of everything our world is screaming at you. The world wants you to believe that you are defined by the answer to *What's next?* The college you attend, the job you land, whether you get married or have kids, how much money you make, how many friends you have, whether you receive any kind of recognition or awards for work or community contributions, whether you can afford to buy a nice house...according to our world, those things don't just determine if you're successful or how much worth or value you possess; they actually define who you are. As if you, your soul, your actual *being* were not separate from what you *do*. The world says they are one and the same. So the answer to *What's next?* really matters to our world, because it's how people allow themselves to be defined and how they allow their worth to be determined.

But you, my friend, know better. All my life, I've heard my dad say over and over, "Don't let the world teach you theology," meaning don't let the world teach you what to believe about God. If we allow the world to teach us about God, we will have the most messed-up, incorrect, contradictory view of Him. It wouldn't be even remotely close to the truth. In the same way, don't let the world teach you who you are. Not just because it'll be wrong, but because the world's over-arching message to you and me is that we aren't enough.

Marketing and advertising agencies spend billions of dollars a year to convince us that we are lacking or in need of something that will make our lives better or make us a better version of our-selves. And it's not just the marketers who tell us that. Our entire culture is built on the idea that what you do with your life, where you live, what job you have, and how much money you make de-fine your identity and worth. It is an insatiable lie, one that most people will go to their grave believing.

But we don't let the world teach us theology, and we don't let the world teach us who we are. The only source of truth we can trust to teach us those things is God's Word. Your identity and value are determined by one thing alone: your Heavenly Father.

Let me briefly remind you what His Word says about you:

- You were made in the image of God. You carry His like-ness. (See Genesis 1:26–27.)
- You are wonderfully made! (See Psalm 139:14.)
- You are His masterpiece and were created for a purpose, already planned by Him! (See Ephesians 2:10.)
- You were chosen. (See 1 Peter 2:9.)
- You are loved. (See 1 John 3:1.)
- You are forgiven. (See Isaiah 1:18 and Ephesians 1:7.)
- He delights in you. (See Psalm 18:19.)
- You have been adopted as his child. (See Romans 8:15 and Ephesians 1:5.)
- He has made you into a new creation. (See 2 Corinthi-ans 5:17.)

The bottom line is this: Your Heavenly Father created you and He loves you. He determines your worth and value through Jesus. Jesus did for you what you could never do for yourself, which is earn God's approval and affection. When you placed your faith in Christ, Jesus covered you. His Spirit indwelled your body. That, and that alone, is your identity.

That is the only identity that will ever satisfy. It is the only way to determine your true worth and value—which will not ever change or spoil. And all of it has nothing to do with what you *do*.

So when you find yourself stressing over **What's next?** take a deep breath and remind yourself that while it is great to plan and create goals, it never, ever will define who you are. Get your nose in God's Word to refill your mind with His truth about who He says you are and what you are worth.

He loves you. He has great plans for you—plans He has already worked out and prepared in advance. You just need to keep your eyes on Him and walk into those plans. That doesn't mean it'll always be easy or look like you want it to. Oftentimes, as Christians, we mistake the "good plans" God has for us with "plans that will make us happy." But it doesn't quite work like that. God has your very best in mind all the time. Yet if He gave us only what we think we want and made us happy, we would never grow. We would never trust Him more. In fact, when life is going our way, we don't really think we even need God. It's when life is hard and we're in the trenches—only then do we remember how desperately we need Him.

So don't mistake hardship or disappointment as God trying to steer you away from something. Don't believe the lie that because hardships occur He must not have your best in mind. Again, that's letting the world teach you theology. And the Bible tells us otherwise!

So trust Him. Keep your eyes on Him. Keep your nose in His Word, your heart aligned with His Spirit, and your life filled with His people. If you keep those things a priority, the *What's next?* will fall into place. I promise.

ACKNOWLEDGMENTS

You might imagine the book-writing process as a lone man on an island. Perhaps that is some authors' experience, but it could not be further from mine. This book would never have come to fruition if it had not been for several people who cheered, inspired, and led me down the path.

First, I would be remiss not to thank all of the college women who wrote me emails, submitted questions through my blog, and walked into my office with their open hearts and issues of the day. Thank you for being the brave ones to ask the questions that we now get to share with so many others wondering the very same things! This book truly would not exist without you.

To my parents, who raised me to believe that God gave me a unique skill set and abilities, and that it wasn't an insane idea to imagine writing a book someday. You instilled a confidence within me that has propelled me to tackle so many obstacles, including this book. To my husband, who always encouraged, always supported, and never hesitated to give me the time or space I needed to work on this project. A special thank-you to Hannah and Lance, who will laugh to see their names on this page, but who connected me to the best agent on the planet, without whom this book would never have seen the light of day. Bryan Norman, I will never forget the first time we spoke on the phone. You believed in this book and understood me in a way no other agent had. Thanks for taking a chance on me and ultimately making this crazy dream of mine come true! Also a huge thank-you to Virginia Bhashkar for the hours and hours you pored over my manuscript, and to all in the FaithWords and Hachette team who made this book a reality. It truly took a village, and I am eternally grateful to my village.

NOTES

CHAPTER FOUR

1 Nicole L. Mihalopoulos, Peggy Auinger, and Jonathan D. Klein, "The Freshman 15: Is It Real?" *Journal of American College Health* 56, no. 5 (2008): 531–533.

2 "Alcohol Calorie Counter," Rethinking Drinking, National Institutes of Health, www.rethinkingdrinking.niaaa.nih.gov /tools/Calculators/calorie-calculator.aspx.

3 "Calories Burned in 30 Minutes for People of Three Different Weights," Harvard Health Publishing, Harvard Medical School, www.health.harvard.edu/diet-and-weight-loss/calories -burned-in-30-minutes-of-leisure-and-routine-activities.

CHAPTER SIX

1 "In Brief," *The Knot Yet Report*, the National Marriage Project at the University of Virginia, the National Campaign to Prevent Teen and Unplanned Pregnancy, and the Relate Institute, http://twentysomethingmarriage.org/in-brief/.

2 Sofus Attila Macskássy, "From Classmates to Soulmates," Facebook Data Science Team, October 7, 2013, https://www .facebook.com/notes/facebook-data-science/from-classmates -to-soulmates/10151779448773859.

CHAPTER SEVEN

1   Robin Hattersley-Gray, "Sexual Assault Statistics," *Campus Safety*, March 5, 2012, www.campussafetymagazine.com /article/Sexual-Assault-Statistics-and-Myths.

2   One in Four, "Sexual Assault Statistics," http://www.oneinfourusa .org/statistics.php.

3   Ibid.

4   "At What Age Is the Brain Fully Developed?" *Mental Health Daily*, February 18, 2015, http://mentalhealthdaily.com /2015/02/18/at-what-age-is-the-brain-fully-developed/.

5   "Support for College Students with Depression," Fountain House College Re-Entry, http://collegereentry.org/depression.

6   Gregg Henriques, "The College Student Mental Health Crisis," *Psychology Today*, February 15, 2014, www.nami.org/Press -Media/Press-Releases/2004/Mental-Illness-Prolific-Among -College-Students.

CHAPTER EIGHT

1   Sticky Faith, Fuller Youth Institute, http://stickyfaith.org.

CHAPTER NINE

1   "Major Exploration," Career Services, University of La Verne, https://sites.laverne.edu/careers/what-can-i-do-with-my-major/.

2   Heather Long, "The New Normal: 4 Job Changes by the Time You're 32," *CNN Money*, April 12, 2016, http://money.cnn.com/2016/04/12/news/economy/millennials-change-jobs-frequently/index.html.

3   Allison Kade, "Nine Things Everyone Should Be Able To Do by Age 30," *Business Insider*, December 17, 2012, www.businessinsider.com/know-how-to-do-these-things-by-age-30-2012-12.

ABOUT THE AUTHOR

Fo over ten years, **Hanna Easley Seymour** has mentored young women, helping them transition smoothly from high school to college and beyond. She holds a BA in interdisciplinary social sciences from James Madison University and an M.Ed. in higher education and student affairs from the University of South Carolina. Combining faith with a passion for helping others, Hanna explains how to tackle problems with good sense and grace on her website, HannaSeymour.com.